Tony Collins has worke Stoughton, Kingsway, Monarch, Lion Hudson and SPCK. Over the course of his career he has published at least 1,400 books, and owned three magazines. He is the recipient of a Lifetime Achievement Award from the Association of Christian Writers.

'One of the most fascinating books I've read in a long time: a wonderfully revealing journey into the mysterious world of publishing, packed full of insights, highs, lows, and anecdotes from Tony's decades working in the industry.'

Dr Andy Bannister, Director, Solas

'Quite frankly, Tony Collins' work is a sheer delight. His writing is crisp, clean, and in some cases quite beautiful. He shares with the reader not only an amazing career – lifetime, really – surrounded by books and writers. He also manages to convey the heart of a patient, kindly, and very passionate gentleman. A marvellous achievement. Highly recommended.'

Davis Bunn, international bestselling author

'If you read books, write them, sell them, or are simply curious, then this book will captivate you from beginning to end. My first meeting with Tony Collins was to give a ten-minute pitch at a writers' conference. I didn't even know what a "pitch" was but left with his business card in my pocket. I wish I'd had this book in the same pocket back then, for the publishing industry is both amazing and terrifying at the same time. From naive wannabe to author of seven books under Tony's guidance, he deflected my terror with his gracious wisdom, allowing me to be amazed. I speak as one of the author's "wild cards". . . thanks for taking the risk, Tony.'

Catherine Campbell, inspirational speaker, and author of *Journey with Me* (CRT winner of Christian Book of the Year, 2019), *Broken Works Best*, and others.

'Tony Collins gives us a fascinating glimpse into the world of publishing, which leaps straight off the page and into your heart.'

Wendy H. Jones, author, and President of the Scottish Association of Writers

'If you love books and publishing, you'll enjoy this story about a life with words. Tony tells his tale with relish, perspective, and good humour.'

Chip MacGregor, long-time literary agent and former publisher with Time-Warner

'Fascinating . . . a behind-the-scenes look at the making of books and magazines that shaped the lives and faith of thousands. Entertaining and informative.'

Amy Boucher Pye, author, spiritual director, and former editor

They'll Never Read That

How to make mistakes in publishing

Tony Collins

Sarah GRACE PUBLISHING
Dyslexic Friendly

'It was simple, and apparently very successful, except, perhaps, in those cases where it was complicated and an utter failure.'

The Department of Sensitive Crimes, Alexander McCall Smith

'I have written three books, sir, and one of them was even published.'

The Perplexing Theft of the Jewel in the Crown, Vaseem Khan

'I would sue myself for defamation of character if I had the money in the bank.'

Miss, What Does Incomprehensible Mean?, Fran Hill

'I'd been flying by the seat of my pants for so long I was surprised my undies didn't have wings.'

Dark Queen, Faith Hunter

'He dreamed the dream of all those who publish books, which was to have so much gold in your pockets that you would have to employ two people just to hold your trousers up.'

Maskerade, Terry Pratchett

By the same author:

Taking My God for a Walk

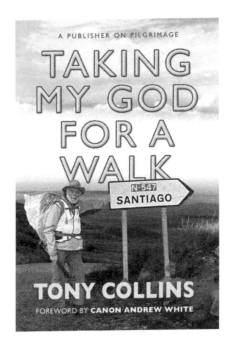

Dedication

To my beloved Pen Wilcock,
source of so much wisdom and laughter.
And to my grandchildren Michael, Ben, Sam, and Iceni.

Contents

Introduction

In the course of several decades, I have made most of the mistakes a publisher can reasonably manage. I have published dozens of unsuccessful books; I have become entangled in a court case; I have launched a magazine which failed dismally; I have allowed my imagination to override my judgement; I have been an enthusiast; I have been a servant of celebrity; I have accepted praise without foundation; I have rejected glittering opportunities; I have overlooked bestsellers; I have given advice I had no business to offer; I have offered unwise encouragement; I have panted along well behind the times.

I have twice been made redundant. Three times I have had the grim task of making others redundant. Publishing is not a stable profession.

I have reprinted books too often.

I offer this in mitigation: I have always loved books, and the crafting of books, and, with one or two exceptions, I have appreciated the company of those who write them.

My chosen field of enterprise is Christian publishing. The wider world of books generally ignores this little universe, which operates to its own set of rules, but it is surprisingly vibrant – remarkably so, given the genteelly moribund nature of much of the Western Church – and its sales can be jaw-dropping. It is far from unknown for Christian books to sell in millions.

Publishing, like bookselling, like teaching, like Christian ministry, attracts people whose abilities could earn them far greater material reward elsewhere. I have had the privilege of working with women and men of intelligence, integrity, wit, and shining humanity.

I have encountered just a few scoundrels, whose faith cloaked a persistent self-interest, but apart from the author, they will probably not appear in this record.

1

A Discovery of Books

One Saturday morning, perhaps seven years old, I selected three books from Horsham Library. That afternoon I returned them, having devoured the lot, and came home with three more.

When I discovered my pocket money, appropriately hoarded, would buy a book, I haunted our local Smiths. Pocket money was set at sixpence – six old pence – a week, and popular books, all hardbacks, were generally priced at 2/6, or half a crown: five sixpences. So, every five weeks, I would bear home Biggles, or Swallows and Amazons, or the works of Willard Price, or a few years later The Saint. On intervening Saturdays I would hang around the shop, sadly underfoot, savouring titles and weighing my next selection.

The book tables at jumble sales became an oasis; second-hand bookshops a destination; our local library a refuge in all seasons, where a bookish child might wander entranced for hours.

My parents were both teachers, and the house was well supplied with bookcases my father had made. They laid down no rules about what I might choose, trusting to their own good taste, and glad to have a son who enjoyed reading. Books were my gateway to the adult world. By my early teens I was exploring the works of Mary Renault and Anya Seton, Monica Dickens and Somerset Maugham, plunging into history and adventure, struggles for identity and searches for meaning and status, belonging and sexual fulfilment. My imagination grew rampant.

I was not always immersed in books: my father early infected me with a love of fishing, and every weekend in summer was occupied with trips to local ponds and rivers, the car boot full of tackle. Each Friday we would discuss, in careful detail, which location might be fishing well given the weather that week. My father would prepare for carp, or bream: I loved the swiftness and delicacy required for elusive roach or dace – and, very occasionally, managed to bag a chub.

None of which are remotely edible. Most coarse anglers treat their catch carefully (these days barbless hooks are mandatory) and return their fish unharmed.

These twin passions swiftly combined. Arthur Ransome's *Rod and Line*, a classic of angling, became a favourite, as did that wonderful selection *The Fisherman's Bedside Book*, a splendid anthology which introduced me in turn to Thoreau's mystical masterpiece *Walden*.

My schoolwork fed the same fires. English literature became an inexhaustible delight. I toted the Penguin *Metaphysical Poets* everywhere, and still have it.

I am that publisher's pleasure, a book addict. I usually have several books on the go, and habitually consume two or three a week. I think, at heart, I became a publisher myself because I could read to the point of satiation, and get paid for it.

At fourteen I became a Christian. It was the culmination of a process. One day, when I was about ten, an invitation dropped through our door from the local Crusaders group (Crusaders was a Bible class, for boys or girls, now rechristened Urban Saints). Years earlier I had been alarmed by Sunday school and refused to attend (each week a child was required to recite the Lord's Prayer, which I couldn't master, and I quit before my turn came round). Crusaders, however, I enjoyed: run by men I admired, who took their faith seriously, it featured whole-hearted singing, good talks, and accessible Bible study. Each summer I attended a Crusader camp, and at one of these I made a commitment: in the language of this culture, I gave my life to Christ.

I was serious about my faith, between lapses, and took to reading my Bible with determination. As a languages student I thought I might combine my fields of study, and my father was amused one morning to discover me sound asleep, light still on, head pillowed on a German New Testament.

Christian books became a revelation, and sometimes a pitfall. I admired Billy Graham, but his *Peace with God*, a multimillion bestseller, completely failed to impress – altogether too saccharine, to a student of English – and quickly found its way to the Out pile. This developing arrogance would trip me repeatedly. Another bestseller, *The Cross and the Switchblade*, became a firm favourite, and my copy fell to pieces with handling. A book for teenage boys on growing as a Christian, which advised me not to consider going out with girls until I was ready to marry, caused considerable grief, and subsequent rebellion.

A work on the careful theology behind the 1968 encyclical *Humanae Vitae*, read with the encouragement of a Catholic girlfriend, impressed me immensely, to the point where I nearly converted. Its simple red dustjacket was part of my beach kit for one entire Mediterranean summer.

Milton's *Paradise Lost* had a profound bearing on my developing Christian cosmology: his dramatic Satan, arrogant and self-obsessed, but vibrant and disturbingly alive, formed part of my imaginative landscape. Milton wrote to justify the ways of God to man, but this was not the whole of his achievement.

In my teens I came across the theological writings of C.S. Lewis (I wouldn't discover his novels until much later) and plunged into *Mere Christianity*, *The Four Loves* and *The Problem of Pain*. His *Screwtape Letters* accompanied me during a year spent teaching in France: I wrote copious notes, longer than the book. His *Letters to Malcolm, Chiefly on Prayer* joined me on a tour of Greece.

My faith, a wavering flame, flickered in the crosscurrents of French surrealism, the poetry of Thomas Hardy, politics, rock music, youthful angst and youthful horniness. I was rescued from complete apostasy by Christian books. As a student I discovered Francis Schaeffer's *Escape from Reason* and *The God Who Is There*, and Ole Hallesby's *Prayer*, a fine publication from the 1930s. All three are still readily available: Christian books can have a long shelf life.

One hot summer, during the university vacation, I obtained a job with Horsham brick works, checking lorries in and out. The experience extended my education. During my lunch hour I was reading Hallesby one day when a driver wandered by.

'What's he doing to her now?' he grinned.

I turned the distinctive red and black cover in his direction. Shocked, he disappeared.

A few days later a driver strode into the office effing and blinding, quite incoherent with rage. When we had calmed him down sufficiently, we learned the incident which had so upset him was that he had been required to deliver bricks to a vicarage. He was mortified. It was as if someone had accused him of having a boyfriend, or voting Conservative.

I cannot remember who recommended it, but I was captivated by Roy Hession's *The Calvary Road*.

Roy Hession was born in London in 1908 and came to faith through the influence of a cousin, a Navy officer. In 1947 he came into contact with Christians involved in the East Africa revival. The experience was to have a profound impact on his life, and it was from this encounter that the message of *The Calvary Road* emerged in 1950.

This little book – scarcely more than a pamphlet – is a brief essay on how God wishes to bless us abundantly, once we acknowledge him as our source of abundance; how walking in the light, and freedom, are outcomes of keeping our eyes on Jesus.

The Calvary Road is a gem. No one knows how many millions it has sold. It has been translated into at least eighty languages. When the distinguished author Pastor Richard Wurmbrand and his wife Sabrina were both languishing in Romanian prisons in the 1950s, their young son Mihai was welcomed and sheltered by courageous members of the underground church. Mihai recorded later how he encountered *samizdat* publishing during those years – sections of the Bible painstakingly copied out by hand, each precious document handed on from one believer to the next. It was intensely risky. Anyone caught with such material risked execution or a long sentence. Along with the Bible, noted Mihai, one other book was perilously copied and distributed: *The Calvary Road.*

Hession's small volume is simple, and starkly written. It has few striking turns of phrase. It neither amuses nor entertains. But truth resides within it, and stirs the heart. I remember sitting in my parents' dining-room one day, having reached the end of the book, looking out over the garden, and realising that my life had been set onto a new path. I felt as if I were coming to my senses for the first time; as if the world had come into focus. It led directly to my realising that the girl from whom I had recently parted was someone I wanted to see again. Jane and I would be married for over thirty years.

If a Christian book could have such an impact . . . *The Calvary Road*, more than any other, would set me on the track towards publishing. In due course I graduated from Exeter University, with a degree in English and French. A keen environmentalist from my teens, I thought a life concerned with the human impact on the natural world might constitute a worthy ambition, and slightly to my surprise – I was the sole candidate on the course with an arts background – I was accepted at Nottingham University to study for an MA in town planning. (The long train journey to the interview from Exeter was eye-opening: I had hardly travelled north of the Thames, and had an image of the Midlands, derived in part from a sloppy reading of D.H. Lawrence, as essentially one vast slag heap. But there were *trees*.)

The course itself rapidly corrected any vapid dreams. I could do the work easily enough, but the insistence on computer programming, and the early forms of computer modelling, left this book-lover cold: the tools proved uncongenial. The material was interesting and obviously important, but at a visceral level I knew I had made the wrong decision. As a schoolboy, years earlier, I had committed the same unrealistic error, selecting sciences over arts when the choice was required, then half a term later switching back to the warmer and more engaging world of languages and humanities.

Years later – having started my own business – I would discover a modest head for figures, a necessary component of publishing. If someone had demonstrated at that early stage how numbers tell the story, I might have stuck with the town planning. And be a lot wealthier.

After two terms of misery at Nottingham I returned home. My parents had been immensely supportive, financing my studies and encouraging my dreams, but when I mused about an academic career, my father put his foot down. Go and find a job, he instructed. You can stay here as long as you wish. Come back to your studies later if you want. But it's time you stopped being a student.

The reasoning went this way: I read incessantly. I am a Christian. Can I combine the two?

I wrote to publishers of Christian books. Paternoster. IVP. Kingsway. Marshall, Morgan & Scott. William Collins. Several more. I stressed my credentials as a student of literature and a believer.

Most ignored me. In my naivety I had not appreciated that nobody walks in off the street to become an editor, nor that publishing generates few vacancies, as staff turnover is low. The larger firms had graduate entry schemes, for which places were highly contested, but of this I knew nothing.

One morning, however, the phone rang. I didn't recognise the caller's cultured tones. After a few moments' conversation Edward England – without question the leading publisher of Christian books in the UK at the time – invited me to an interview at Hodder & Stoughton, in London.

Gosh.

Hodder & Stoughton was founded in 1868 by Matthew Henry Hodder and Thomas Wilberforce Stoughton, two evangelical laymen who had the vision of providing books for the increasingly literate masses. Combining astute judgement and considerable publishing experience, the two laid the foundations for an imprint that still flourishes today. Initially they published only religious and nonfiction works, though as the company expanded, these parameters relaxed.

At this point – 1974 – Hodder was still privately owned. It was a considerable enterprise, publishing a vast range of prestigious authors including John le Carré, John Creasey, David Niven, Anthony Sampson, Jean M. Auel, and many more. For a century the religious output had been a steady component in Hodder's output, notably under the formidable editor Leonard Cutts, who also edited the Teach Yourself series. Now it was under the care of the even more formidable Edward England.

Edward had managed the prestigious Scripture Union bookshop in London's Wigmore Street. In 1966 he obtained a position with Hodder & Stoughton, working under Cutts. Edward's early years at Hodders featured some impressive achievements, including the swift and successful editing of *Impossible Voyage*, the autobiography of yachtsman and former paratrooper Chay Blyth. In 1971 Blyth became the first person to sail non-stop westwards (against prevailing winds and currents) around the world. As Blyth finally entered Plymouth harbour, Edward was there to meet him and, expertly overseen, the book appeared that November.

When Leonard Cutts retired, he took Edward to one side and privately advised him to ignore the Christian list, which had once been central to the company's output. But Edward had other ideas. Asked by Hodder's management what he wanted to do, he responded: rebuild the religious programme. Within a year he had signed up not only the Bible translator J.B. Phillips, whose testimony *Ring of Truth* would sell over 250,000 copies, but also the astonishing story of Richard Wurmbrand, the Romanian pastor mentioned above.[1] Edward then obtained a licence to publish the fantastically popular The Living Bible. Edward

---

1. Wurmbrand's autobiography *Tortured for Christ* would bring to the world's attention the suffering of Christians in Eastern Europe, selling several million copies and being translated into at least twenty-three languages.

had the Touch. Shortly thereafter, he was invited to join Hodder's main board.

A member of his staff had recently quit. He needed an assistant. When he offered me a temporary position for six weeks, I accepted with alacrity.

At that point I had completed a degree; I had passed driving tests for moped, motorbike and car; I had spent a year teaching in France; I had hitch-hiked right across Europe and down to the far coast of Sicily. I had been an evangelist on the streets of Geneva. I was engaged to be married. I could sit up straight, eat a meal without tossing chicken bones over my shoulder or blowing my nose on the tablecloth, and speak halting German, passable French and impeccable BBC English.

When it came to life, business and publishing, I didn't have a clue.

2

Acutely Green

Edward must have been slightly horrified at the wide-eyed innocent he had acquired, but he persevered. On my first morning he leafed through the dozen or so letters that had arrived, shoved them into my hands, showed me to a corner desk (very much the low place on the totem pole, right next to the incessantly flapping swing doors), barked a few instructions and told me to reply to them all and show him what I had done.

I looked around. Busy, competent people were doing complex incomprehensible things and holding conversations I couldn't follow.

To start with, I couldn't type, and typing was required. Edward had taught himself: as a young man he had been a journalist, a profession where fast accurate copy was an absolute necessity, and he had learned to type with two fingers. He habitually attacked the little portable in his office (chocked with books to stop it escaping) with such ferocity – punching out seventy words a minute – that if you held a page of his work up to the window, light streamed through all the 'o's. In those days any office resounded to the clacking of typewriter keys. When Edward was busy at his machine, the entire floor was aware.

I quickly realised I was painfully incapable, and there was no question of secretarial services for this junior oik. Bravely, and in retrospect cheekily, I asked if the company would pay for me to undertake some training. For an hour after work, for three weeks, I followed an intensive touch-typing course in Oxford Street, and emerged with a certificate that optimistically confirmed my competence. It would prove one of the most useful skills I ever learned.

I had read many hundreds of books, but I had no idea how a book came to being. Royalties, contracts, market sectors, stock control, marketing and selling, discount structures and all the arcana of the world of print, paper, design and typography: so much to learn. Each area had its specialists, but an editor (the generalist of the publishing world) needed to know something of them all. Then there were matters more strictly editorial: readership, structure, subheads, flow, indexes, libel, copyright, permissions, the merits of anecdote, the art of cover copy – an entire litany of esoteric aspects for which years of literature studies had failed to equip me.

Today an aspiring graduate looking to enter the industry will probably undertake an MA in publishing: there are many good options. In 1974 no such course existed. You learned on the job. Women started as secretaries; men as salesmen. Both positions gave a decent grounding. As I later discovered, I was the first editor to come in off the street in Hodder's history, and fitted no mould. I would be offered no formal training, beyond a visit to a printing plant. I was an awkward anomaly, and utterly, acutely green.

This was brought sharply home to me when, after a couple of weeks, Edward dropped on my desk the typescript of what would prove a seminal book: *When the Spirit Comes* by Colin Urquhart.

'Write a cover wording,' he instructed. 'Come and show me when you're done.'

Head down, I started reading. An hour and a half later he appeared at my desk. 'Aren't you finished yet?' he demanded. Scanning my miserable notes, he shook his head. 'You haven't got a clue. Come with me.'

Back in his office he swung a spare chair over to his desk and gestured me to sit. 'Start with something arresting,' he instructed, leafing through the opening pages. 'This is a great story, and at the heart of it is a healing ministry.' I nodded: I'd grasped that much. 'Find a good phrase, and build your blurb around it.' The table juddered and the little portable rattled as he pounded at the keys. 'Here you are,' he told me, cranking round the roller. *'Something different was needed; not just praying for sick people, but healing them!* That will work,' he added. 'It tells the charismatics this book is for them.

'Now set the scene for your reader,' he instructed, typing away. *'When the Reverend Colin Urquhart began his ministry as parish priest of St Hugh's, near Luton, on a large housing estate, he knew from the experience of his predecessors that life would be . . .'* He paused and looked at me.

'Demanding?'

He shook his head. 'Too many syllables, too weak.' The keys blurred briefly. *'Tough.'*

'Now for the meat,' he continued. 'Keep it short and sharp . . . *Within four years, however, his church had changed beyond recognition as the members found themselves witnessing miracles of healing, and establishing new relationships with one another, as God gave them a remarkable vision of love, community, and service.'*

He sat back and beamed at me. 'That's all you need. Count the words.'

A pause. 'Eighty-six.'

He nodded, satisfied. In the space of a few minutes he had created a piece of succinct, arresting copy. 'The shorter the better,' he told me, jabbing the paper for emphasis. 'Long blurbs just mean the editor hasn't grasped the essence.'

I learned rather a lot that day. Narrative holds the attention, so use it to captivate. Send clear signals to potential readers. Focus on what really matters. And – critically – connect to the topic of the moment. At that juncture the charismatic renewal, arguably the biggest upheaval in the Church since the Reformation, was getting into gear, and was tapping into a profound hunger for *something more* (a phrase which would, a year or two later, become the title of a bestselling book by Catherine Marshall). The upsurge in faith that had followed the Second World War was dying away, and Christians of all stripes were looking for the immediate and authentic. Healing, and more generally miracles – 'signs and wonders' – were characteristics of the movement. Colin Urquhart, a shy but determined young priest from the Anglo-Catholic end of the ecclesiastical spectrum, would become a key figure.

I learned something further. An avid reader, I thought my reading speed was pretty good. Edward expected better. He could consume, grasp, and (frequently) discard books at a rattling pace, and demanded the same of me. I never did learn to speed-read, which is a different skill, but I gradually improved.

Early on he gave me a piece of invaluable advice: 'Don't spend time on books you're not going to publish.' Hodders was, and remains, a leader in the field of Christian publishing, and attracted hopeful authors from across the world. Each post brought its quota of new submissions, and every morning Edward would pass me a pile of typescripts to assess and (almost without exception) turn down.

'You haven't got time to read them,' he snapped, coming past my desk an hour into one absorbing morning. 'Sniff 'em. If they don't smell right, turn them down. No publisher ever went broke by turning books down.'

Speed is a survival skill in publishing, and before long I did indeed learn to 'sniff' – to test whether the first few pages held the attention, to flick through the text to check for breadth of vocabulary and use of English, to scrutinise the contents for originality and pertinence, and check the author's authority and profile.

The first few rejection letters included an explanation, but after I was drawn into a tricky exchange, Edward quickly set me straight.

'You don't have time to get into correspondence,' he insisted. 'Tell them something true, but make sure they can't argue about it.'

'Dear Sir, Dear Madam,' I learned to respond. 'Thank you for your proposal. Unfortunately, we have recently released a book on a similar topic . . . we are currently receiving far more submissions than we can publish . . . the commercial potential of your book would not meet our criteria . . . we only publish Christian titles and your book would not be well received in our market sector . . . we do not publish poetry . . . this would be better suited to an academic list . . . the cost of the copyright material you have included would make publication difficult . . .'

These responses were fair, accurate, hard to dispute, and deliberately incomplete. There is nothing to be gained by telling an author that their book is boring, their use of English shoddy, their theology incoherent, their ideas derivative, their support base non-existent, their obsession with the Second Vatican Council not widely shared, and no one has heard of them, so their autobiography is unlikely to be of interest.

As I grew a little more confident in this almost daily exercise, I added another consideration: kindness. Even the worst book is someone's brainchild. An author has spent months, perhaps years, in its preparation. From their perspective it's as good as it can be. They have poured themselves into the task. It is a daunting matter to put your literary baby into the hands of a stranger, an exercise festooned with potential for humiliation and disappointment. I decided it was not part of my job to make any author feel worse about themselves, and started to search for warmer phrases which did not admit of argument: 'We have a very full list for the next year . . . We would not be able to do justice to your material . . .' These days, with the rise of self-publishing and the services of Amazon, I have often added a little candid guidance: 'You will see a better return if you publish privately.'

I learned one further wrinkle, as time went by. Many publishers operate some form of 'slush pile' system, where prospective typescripts are parked until the junior editor has time to go through them. Authors often wait months for a response, which is aggravating and disheartening. I decided I would strive to turn books down with all possible despatch. It's not always easy or possible, but this is a resolution I have done my best to keep.

People aren't stupid, and if your truth is not the whole truth then an author will know. But you have given a clear signal, and that matters.

After three weeks Edward left for a business trip to visit publishers in the States. 'You're in charge,' he told me cheerfully. 'I'll be away for ten days. Turn everything down. Dictate your letters to my secretary. She'll keep a copy of every letter you write. I want a clear desk when I get back.'

The following Monday I went through the mail, took a deep breath, and – like the rudderless dinghy I was – floundered out into the deep, representing to authors across the world the venerable, prestigious house of Hodder. What could go wrong?

These days the position of *secretary* has almost disappeared from the publishing world, and indeed from most other enterprises: swallowed up in the advance of email and cost-cutting. Back in the seventies, to have your own PA was a matter of some prestige, and a competent secretary did a great deal to enhance the reputation of the (usually male) executive.

Edward's secretary, Mrs Hunt, was a formidable creature; a bewigged lady of middle years with a truculent attitude and a keen mind. She thought less than nothing of taking dictation from a callow youth barely old enough to be her son, but with an air of one making the best of it, decided to do what was necessary to protect her boss from his inadequate assistant. However, my grammar was accurate, and my English teachers had drummed into me the concept of one idea per paragraph, so I knew how to craft a letter. After a rocky few days, we fell into a routine: I'd go through the mail and dictate responses; she would argue with my decisions and suggest alternative phraseology. Gradually we would reach an accommodation.

All went well until the day a typescript arrived from Canada. I made the mistake of starting to read it, and was quickly hooked by its erudition, felicitous quotations, spiritual depth, and the author's genial personality. I tried a few samples on Mrs Hunt, who responded positively. Convinced I had stumbled across a work of luminous spirituality, I replied enthusiastically to the author.

A week later, Edward returned, and one of his first acts was to whiffle though the stack of carbon copies. Half an hour later he materialised at my desk, the offending letter ripped from the wodge of paper and stapled to the typescript. 'Not a chance,' he said crisply. 'The author's not a Christian, in the sense our market will understand. No one's heard of him. Canada's a tricky territory. It's too long. The quotations would cost a fortune. You did exactly what I told you not to do. Turn it *down*.'

Edward's scorn was withering. Gulping and red-faced, I set to work to retract my earlier praise without implying that Hodders had employed a complete prat.

Worse was to follow. A few days later my phone rang. The Canadian author had received my original letter, and had been so cheered by my response he had jumped on a plane to London and was now in reception. Clearly my follow-up missive hadn't arrived in time. Panicking, I barged into Edward's office seeking advice. He grinned at me. 'You'll have to explain in person,' he observed unsympathetically.

The four flights down to reception were the longest set of stairs I had ever descended. An elderly, dignified gentleman greeted me warmly. As I stumbled through my incoherent explanation, his cheerful countenance fell. With a restraint that cut more deeply than anger, he thanked me for my time, silently donned his coat and hat, and left.

Hodders had indeed employed a prat. That acutely uncomfortable episode taught me more caution than I had managed to accumulate in twenty-four years. In publishing, enthusiasm is a luxury.

The six weeks pounded past. A few days before my time was up, Edward called me into his sanctum. I had been expecting this conversation and sat down, rubbing my sweaty hands on the knees of my cheap suit. Apart from the poor Canadian, there had been a host of other errors. I was conscious of my status as office liability. I so badly wanted to be a publisher. I prayed silently and incoherently.

That morning, unsure of what lay ahead, I had stood in front of the Army recruiting office near Charing Cross. For long minutes I had stared at the seductive posters, weighing my options. They were looking for graduates. How would Jane, my fiancée, feel about being an Army wife?

Her Majesty's Forces stood no chance. The world of books had my soul in its grip.

There was an excruciating pause.

'You're doing ok,' Edward said slowly, looking at me hard. 'We thought you knew more than you did. But you're a worker. And you've got an eye for detail. We've decided to extend your contract for six months.'

Sweet Lord Almighty. I might yet have a career.

My first task each morning was to read through Edward's carbon copies, his correspondence from the day before. This was a delight. I didn't clearly realise it, but I was being given a masterclass in publishing. Urbane, precise, concise, sometimes sharp but always courteous, his letters – rarely longer than a side of A4 – opened to me a world of sophisticated and subtle judgement. He was patient, meticulous, crisp, and oh so shrewd.[2] Gracefully phrased epistles explained to highly successful writers why their new book needed further work. A cheerful and affectionate piece to an old acquaintance might trail a new

---

2. When Edward was first appointed, as he described in his autobiography *An Unfading Vision*, he had asked God for the gift of discernment: 'to recognise men on whom Christ had laid hold'.

idea across the recipient's path. Elegant brief approaches to a newly minted bishop, or to the latest *enfant-terrible*-turned-believer, played their part in building the programme. Occasionally teeth emerged: to a laggardly publishing director in the States, he once wrote, 'Dear Steve, If you are dead, please would your successor reply to this note?'

Publishing, I gradually realised, was largely about people. Leading Christian authors turned to Hodders not so much because of the company's stellar reputation, but because Mr England would be their editor.

Instead, increasingly, they got me. Edward believed in the deep-end approach to management, and from that point on he did not hesitate to thrust text after text into my hands. 'Go through it and write a report,' he'd instruct. 'I want it on my desk by tomorrow.' By tomorrow, I quickly discovered, another volume would be waiting. Books of prayers, works of liberation theology, biographies and personal testimonies, Catholics and evangelicals, charismatics and liberals: Hodders published them all, and soon many were passing across my desk. I am sure Edward vetted every detail in those early days, but it felt risky and exhilarating: I was *editing*. I felt immensely alive.

An immediate benefit of the job was access to the Hodder current and back catalogue. With Edward's encouragement, I set to work to cram into my brain as many books as possible, scrounging samples, inspecting returns in the warehouse before they were sent for pulping, swimming with open mouth like a whale shark through shoals of books. It was heaven. The bookshelves at home filled and overflowed. My universe expanded: there was so much to discover.

Faced with endless possibilities, I elected to concentrate on the long tradition of Christian books. Early on Edward recommended that I explore the work of his friends the co-authors John and Elizabeth Sherrill, a professional writing couple whose sales were calculated in millions: *The Hiding Place, The Happiest People on Earth, God's Smuggler, The Cross and the Switchblade*. Transfixed by *The Hiding Place*, the story of the Dutch lady Corrie ten Boom, who hid Jews from the Nazis, I managed in the course of one day to miss several trains, standing engrossed on the platform as the 4.52 drew in, then pulled away. This has always seemed to me to set a benchmark for any writer: to write so compellingly that your readers miss their connection.

One of the joys, and hypocrisies, of publishing is that you have to navigate alien seas, far out of sight of land. Every book is different. Successful and distinguished authors come from every class and background, and tend to assume a competent editor will have a working knowledge of their specialism. Writers expect advice, intelligent guidance, a sounding board rather than an empty vessel. This is all the more true as self-publishing becomes a viable option: if you're not getting competence, why use a publisher? The editor faces a strong temptation to impress: to imply, or more foolishly to assume, you know more than you do.

I started to discover these deeper waters a few weeks later. Working on F.W. Dillistone's magisterial biography of the polymath theologian Charles Raven, it occurred to me that there might not yet be a decent biography of the distinguished New Testament specialist C.H. Dodd. Professor Dodd had died the previous year. Might Dr Dillistone tell his life story?

Dr F.W. Dillistone was an elegant, erudite scholar. I only met him a couple of times, but remember him as an elderly, poised, gracious man. He had spent the greater part of his life in theological education, and was now retired from his last post as Fellow and Chaplain at Oriel College, Oxford. He was intimately familiar with the theological world, its rapids and treacherous undertows. He had written many books.

From Edward's perspective, to my surprise, my erratic arrow landed on target.

'Great idea,' he responded. 'Just the man for the job. Write to Dillistone. Explain what you have in mind. We'll need to know the number of words, and when he can complete it.' He grinned at me. 'You'd better say you have my full support.' To my surprise and appreciation, he added a note to the weekly in-house news sheet, reporting that Tony had commissioned his first book. He might have said 'had laid his first egg', so great was my sense of shock.

It was some time before I connected the dots.

Publishing, as I mentioned, was not Edward's first career. After a stint working for a northern newspaper, he had joined Scripture Union as a bookshop manager, taking up the running of the prestigious Wigmore Street shop in central London in 1957, at the age of just twenty-seven.

The nine years he spent there developed his remarkable instinct for what people wanted to read, and gave early indication of his capacity for the bold stroke. When the New English Bible, New Testament, was published in 1961, he ordered 2,000 copies, prompting a call from OUP's head office to check if he was serious. Every shop in London sold out on the day of publication, with a single exception, and Edward took great delight in supplying stock, at a modest discount, to the other booksellers of the capital. In later years he would calculate print runs by working out what he would have ordered at Wigmore Street, and multiplying by ten.

C.H. Dodd had overseen the translation of the New English Bible. No wonder Edward backed this tribute.

Dr Dillistone was graciousness itself, responding in his impeccable handwriting (he was one of the very few authors who would still turn in a *manuscript*, in the strict sense) and cheerfully agreeing to my proposal. I am sure he realised he was dealing with an editor younger than many of his students, but I pretended to know what I was doing, and he handled the matter with immense good will, mailing the precious finished article well within the time limit. Luckily for me – whose knowledge of theology was sketchy, to say the least – the book required little intervention.

It would complete a pleasing narrative arc if I could report that *C.H. Dodd, Interpreter of the New Testament* sailed through a dozen reprints and became regarded as a classic of its kind. Sadly, not: it failed to sell its modest first printing, and was remaindered.

Publishers always learn more from their failures than their successes. Looking back, I think the whole idea was mistaken. Professor Dodd was, in some circles, justly famous, but those circles were relatively small. More critically, he had spent his entire life within the academic world, and Dr Dillistone, for all his narrative skill, had too slight a story to tell.

It was still my first book.

Edward's publishing programme in those years was pretty much gold. Hodder & Stoughton's Christian output in the early 1970s included exceptional authors such as Michael Green, David Watson, Corrie ten Boom, Catherine Marshall, Richard Wurmbrand, Francis Schaeffer, Cliff Richard, Malcolm Muggeridge, Archbishop Donald Coggan, Cardinals Heenan and Hume, Colin Urquhart, John and Elizabeth Sherrill, Michael Harper, and Jackie Pullinger. The figures were astonishing: for one sales conference Edward asked me to compile sales for some of the leading titles, many of which had sold 60,000 or more. As one startling number after another flashed up on screen, the salesmen murmured in astonishment, as did the executives.

In addition, Edward set about acquiring a modern Bible translation for Hodders, getting rights to The Living Bible and the New International Version. The latter in particular would prove an enormous acquisition, but more of that anon.

Yet it was only a small part of the whole. Hodder books might rule the Christian seas, but the list was run by three people among a staff of hundreds, with functions such as proofreading, design, and production services provided by the wider company. If we wanted specialist input, we were the specialists.

Under this heading came the design of catalogues and the placing of advertising. Soon after I joined, the autumn catalogues for the year were delivered, and Edward was horrified at the drab, unimaginative document – the black and white cover depicted a lectern – which the marketing department had created for his sparkling list. It was the first example I had seen of the frequent incomprehension which secular marketing executives display when faced with anything religious.

Edward decided to put me in charge of Christian book marketing.

This meant, I discovered, a disconcertingly wide range of functions. Apart from writing and checking the important spring and autumn new books catalogues (and seeking better cover images), I found myself responsible for the Hodder Christian Paperbacks brochure, a spring publication covering the entire religious backlist, featuring hundreds of titles. Price, page extent, title, author, ISBN: all had to be painstakingly checked, which in those pre-digital days meant hauling book after book off the shelf for verification. Didn't this book have two authors? Was that edition still in print? Inflation was rampant: had the price changed? Surely that page extent was wrong? Any error was bound to be spotted by some indignant bookshop manager.

Space advertising added another dimension to my burgeoning responsibilities. Edward would tell me what he wanted to push, and leave me to sort it out. The advertising executives on the *Church Times, Church of England Newspaper, Christian Herald, Baptist Times* and *Methodist Recorder* soon learned I was the person to phone, and very few days went by without some hopeful voice on the end of the line asking if there was anything I would like to promote. 'I see you have a new book by Richard Wurmbrand,' the caller would purr. 'I have a little space left on page eight. I am sure you will recall that we give ten per cent discount to publishers.'

I soon discovered a negotiating tool: extracts. 'Thank you for the opportunity,' I learned to purr back. 'It would be so much easier to justify the expense to my director if an extract from Pastor Wurmbrand's book could appear in the same issue . . .' Advertising managers were more than happy to trade, meeting their budgets with space nabbed from their editorial colleagues.

Copywriting is fun, and I quickly fell into a routine, learning to capture in a few arresting words the unique selling point of a title.

All went well, until one Friday morning Edward called me into his office. I wandered in, unaware, to be confronted by my boss as unsmilingly angry as I had ever seen him. He slapped down on his desk a copy of that week's *Church Times*, folded open to the book pages. 'Tell me what's wrong with that.'

Starting to shake, I scanned our advert. All seemed in order.

'You've advertised the Archbishop's book, but you haven't mentioned the author,' Edward growled. 'I don't know what bothers me more: the fact that you did it or the fact that when I showed it to you, you couldn't see it.

It's the *Church Times*, for heaven's sake. He has certainly noticed it. Go away.'

Blinded by tears, I fled to the gents' loo down the corridor. Bolting the cubicle door I sat down and sobbed as quietly as I could. Publishing depends on good relations, and good relations depend on competence. I had succeeded in embarrassing my boss in the eyes of one of his most distinguished authors. The Archbishop of Canterbury is the second person in the nation, second only to the monarch, and *I had forgotten to mention his name.*

There was no escaping it: I would have to resign.

Except that I couldn't bring myself to do so. I might be a wretched editor, but I loved what I did.

Edward hadn't fired me, not in so many words. I mopped myself up and crept back past his door, which was thankfully closed, and returned to my desk. I waited for the phone call telling me to clear my things, but it didn't come. After a few minutes I went back to the text I was checking. In due course lunchtime arrived, and I mournfully repaired to a bench in St Paul's Square with my sandwich.

That afternoon Edward called me in again. I expected the worst. Standing in front of his desk I did my best to pay attention as he detailed some task he wanted me to undertake. Gradually it dawned on me: if he was giving me work then I still had a job. Stammering, I started to apologise afresh, admitting I had thought of quitting. 'That would be a weakness,' Edward rejoined curtly. 'Everyone makes mistakes. The point is to learn from them.'

It was another of publishing's foundational truths: you cannot see what isn't there. All forms of editing involve checking and rechecking, a tedious exercise, and it is easy to do it mechanically, your eye flitting from detail to detail without truly absorbing what you are seeing. The famous error in what became known as the Adulterer's Bible, or the Wicked Bible, in a reprint of the King James Version in 1631, was created by a compositor who failed to observe that he had omitted the 'not' from Exodus 20:14, thus instructing readers 'Thou shalt commit adultery.' Copies were rounded up and burned; the publishers were heavily fined and deprived of their printing licence.

Of course, this is not just a matter of proofreading. Any book is necessarily selective. Part of the editor's task is to spot the omissions.

A few years back a friend showed me a finely produced book he had been given, pointing out with a grin that it had been published privately: who needed publishers? I admired the cover, the quality paper, the elegant layout. Something struck me. 'This is the author's name,' I mused, 'but who *is* he?'

My friend paused, then started to laugh. The author had failed to consider his readers might need to know something about him. If you are going to spend tens of hours reading a book, it is reasonable to expect some information about your companion on the journey.

Publishers may rise and fall, but the world will always need editors.

The commission to take on religious marketing proved an extraordinary slice of blessing. Over the next few years I found myself pitchforked into one promotional campaign after another.

I was sent to shepherd the author of *Born Again*, Charles Colson, around London. Colson, former hatchet man of disgraced American president Richard Nixon, was a tough Washington lawyer and politico ('the evil genius of an evil administration', wrote journalist David Plotz) who had spent months in prison for obstruction of justice in the wake of the Watergate scandal. His conversion just as he was facing arrest (the result of reading C.S. Lewis's *Mere Christianity*) was seen as an attempt to save his skin, and greeted with hoots of derision by the press on both sides of the Atlantic. The London papers were keen to let more blood from this once-feared top executive, but were not quite sure of what to make of the reformed jailbird. Colson was an undoubted celebrity, and for all his new-minted faith, this acutely intelligent former captain in the US Marines was not a man to treat lightly.

High-profile engagements, of which there were many, were handled by Edward and by the managing director of Hodder & Stoughton, Eric Major, but they were pleased to hand evening events to the office junior. Politicians of all stripes were keen to meet Colson, and I ended up carrying his bag to patrician gatherings around Westminster. My signed copy has survived many book culls.

The effort paid off: we sold over 40,000 hardbacks in the next few months.

Colson, for his part, found compassion along with his faith. The hard man of the Republican Party was horrified and profoundly moved by the conditions and backgrounds of the inmates he had met in prison, and went on to found the influential charity Prison Fellowship International. He would become a prolific author, broadcaster, and public speaker, receiving fifteen honorary doctorates as well as the substantial Templeton Prize for Progress in Religion. In 2008 he was awarded the Presidential Citizens Medal by President George W. Bush.

There is more joy in heaven over one sinner that repenteth. Christians love a good villain.

I learned something else from my time with Colson. Secular media will cover Christian material if the story has genuine meat. By that point in Britain's national life the reputation of the Church was rapidly ebbing. Secular bookstores were notably reluctant to carry Christian books – in consequence, during the 1970s and 1980s the number of Christian bookstores multiplied sharply – and the national press were caught up in the same anticlerical mood I had encountered a few years earlier in Horsham brickworks. It was becoming increasingly hard to place stories in the media. Christianity had become profoundly uncool, in itself no bad thing. Yet, as the Colson experience showed, there were exceptions.

Which is not to say such stories were, or are, handled well or wisely. This applies to all coverage of religion, and the staggering ignorance of both journalists and politicians is both irritating and dangerous. It is quite possible to argue that the aftermath of the Iraq war was made far worse by the inability of senior American and British officials to recognise the importance of working with Iraqi spiritual leaders.

The problem does not go away. The BBC's online news service invites you to personalise your news feed, but offers no option for 'religion'. (Nor for golf, to my irritation.)

With my increased workload, the weeks thundered by. As the sixth month ended Edward again summoned me to his office. 'You're doing ok,' he acknowledged, fixing me with his thousand-yard stare. 'You're still making stupid mistakes' – I winced, wondering which grim detail was to be brought forcibly to my attention – 'but you're learning.' Another excruciating pause. 'We've decided to keep you on for another year.'

I exhaled with relief. Quite apart from the utter fascination of the job, I had an eating habit to maintain, and an impending marriage.

'It's time you learned something new,' Edward continued, handing me a typed list. 'Here are twenty-five accounts I want you to look after. They're all in London. One day a week I want you out of the office, selling to these shops. Make up a sales folder – the sales manager will show you how – and start setting up appointments.'

I didn't realise it then, but my training had intensified sharply. I had been handed a gift: any editor will do their job more effectively if they know what sells. I was about to meet, for the first time, members of that underrated profession, the Christian bookshop manager.

3

On the Road

Any bookshop manager worthy of the title will know about their stock, their customers, and the drivers behind the ebbs and flows of their business. To run a Christian bookshop requires additional skills: a working knowledge of theological pitfalls; a ready supply of recommendations for the odder customer; a capacity to distinguish between the specialist and the nutter; and a pastoral heart which can find space for distressed members of the public whose wandering steps lead to their door. All this, on a miniscule salary.

The accounts Edward had entrusted to my care were diverse, and of high calibre: the London shops of Scripture Union and Christian Literature Crusade; the Protestant Truth Society and the Catholic Truth Society; the leading Anglican bookshop, Church House Bookshop in Westminster; Salvationist Publishing and Supplies; London City Mission; Mowbrays, the venerable bookshop close to All Souls; Foyles' religious section; Westminster Cathedral Bookshop; and a host of smaller accounts, ranging from the assertively evangelical to the genially liberal. Their managers were equally mixed: some were scarcely older than me, but many were senior booksellers, canny and experienced, by no means all believers.

The sales representatives employed by Hodder & Stoughton – among whom I could, by stretching the facts, now count myself – were a skilled, distinctly worldly crew, not without an ingrained patina, but hard-driving and hard-driven. Certain standards were expected, notably the possession of a trilby, not necessarily to wear, but to place on the shop counter as a badge of office.[3]

Lapses were not tolerated. The year I arrived, an indignant manager called the head office to announce they would not be purchasing anything further from Hodders. One of the sales team had been seen driving past the bookshop, *smoking in the car.*

Edward cheerfully assured me none of the reps knew how to spell 'God', but in truth they enjoyed their forays into the Christian accounts. Many of the shops had been established to bring light to those sitting in darkness, but the benighted rarely entered their portals. Once a month, however, the man from Hodders would appear, utterly unsaved, and would be treated to a cup of tea and a chocolate biscuit, leaving with an optimistic order.

Once the bookshops in my care established that a Christian, of all things, was soliciting their custom, their attitude changed. I found myself called to account for all manner of perceived deviations from best practice. This cover featured a stained-glass window, and reeked of Anglicanism, that ancient heresy. Surely I realised the charismatic renewal was an attempt to undermine

---

3. No hat was provided, sadly.

the Bible? Why had this title been postponed? Didn't we appreciate Christians couldn't afford hardbacks? A customer had complained about this illustration – a finger jabbed the page – which suggested the devil was black: were we racists? And the perennially popular: why were Hodder's discounts so low?

On the whole I was treated well, but quickly discovered time was limited, and books ephemeral. Customers were far more valuable than sales people. Experienced booksellers could tell at a glance if a book was likely to be viable, and had little patience with elaborate explanations. After a few weeks I abandoned any attempt to describe the work in detail: my buyers needed headlines. Endorsements mattered, as did forewords. Author profile mattered, so did previous titles. Hodder's reputation could get a new author through the door, but only in ones and twos. A book might take years to write, but you had perhaps thirty seconds before the impatient bookseller flipped to the next page of the folder. 'No . . . no . . . three . . . dreadful cover . . . no.'[4] If a paying customer approached the counter the thread was broken. The purchase complete, the manager would turn back to his or her semi-welcome visitor with an audible sigh and a muttered 'Where were we?' You had to know. I learned to turn on, and suspend, enthusiasm to order.

I knew little about selling, but my inside knowledge of the list proved a true asset, and many of the smaller

---

4. This has not changed. An experienced sales colleague observes, looking at the steady devastation of retail outlets, which accelerated during the COVID pandemic, 'The standard order is "none".' Only a fraction of books published actually find a place on bookshop shelves.

shops had been neglected. A year later I was able to hand Edward a list of annual turnovers for the assorted accounts, showing they had on average doubled in size.

Looking back, that was invaluable experience and excellent training. Every commissioning editor should know how to sell books.

Sales could be fun. But there were bear traps.

One of my more uncomfortable encounters was with Mr Roger Page, manager of the Christian Literature Crusade store in Ave Maria Lane, close to St Paul's Cathedral. CLC was – and is – a worldwide mission, and this prestigious store was their flagship.

Roger Page was a slight, serious individual, a few years older than myself, whose faith was deep and doctrine sharply defined. I quickly discovered what would and would not pass muster. If he was not sure how trustworthy a book might be, he would ask for a copy for vetting. By this process Richard Foster's famous *Celebration of Discipline* was stocked, but only for customers who asked for it: copies were kept beneath the counter and handed over concealed in a paper bag.[5]

Mr Page and I established a rapport, of sorts. I learned the parameters within which he operated, and if he thought a book was God-breathed he would back it strongly. He taught me a lot, and I grew to respect him: he was the only bookshop manager I knew who had the courage, standing at his counter, simply to close his eyes in the middle of a

---

5. CLC was not alone in this. During his years at Scripture Union Edward had – on instruction from SU's directors – given similar treatment to C.S.Lewis's classics *The Problem of Pain* and *The Four Loves*.

conversation and silently pray for guidance before placing an order. He was a man of unswerving integrity.

I came unstuck, however, with a youthwork course from The Salvation Army. At that point Hodder & Stoughton published a popular twice-yearly series of Bible reading notes written by Salvationist authors, entitled *The Soldier's Armoury,* and Edward thought other Army resources might find a market. Their youthwork course was an inoffensive collection of talks and activities. One day, however, I rolled up for my regular meeting to find Mr Page staring at me apologetically but firmly.

'You'll have to take them back,' he informed me, lifting onto the counter a pile of colourful paperbacks.

'What's the problem?' I stammered, entirely rocked: clearly the limited connection I thought we had established was in jeopardy. This was not a light matter. Any sales person seeks to win the trust of clients, and will advise customers with care. I had assumed The Army to be beyond reproach, and had recommended this resource to CLC's youth and children's buyer.

Mr Page thumbed through to the end notes and held the copy out. In the end notes the author had cited a volume by William Barclay.

Months previously I had worked on the course, and had foolishly overlooked this detail. Dr William Barclay, a Scottish theologian and broadcaster, and author of dozens of books, notably the 17-volume *Daily Study Bible* from St Andrew's Press, was widely admired for his clarity, warmth, accessible scholarship, and adroit use of illustration. A year or so before, Hodders had published two successful devotionals: *Through the Year with William*

Barclay and *Every Day with William Barclay*. In my ignorance I had simply accepted him as a distinguished author.

Barclay represented a strand of faith far removed from CLC. He was a universalist, a sceptic concerning the Holy Trinity, and embraced the idea of evolution. To evangelicals he was anathema. Despite his erudition (he had been Professor of Divinity at the University of Glasgow), his presence even in a footnote was too much to accept.

In retrospect it was an obvious error, and I had failed in my duty as an editor – failed not only my employer, but also The Salvation Army, as I should have warned the course's authors. I took the books back, and learned my lesson: footnotes matter. So do boundaries.

This was my first really bruising encounter with unyielding evangelicalism. I had come to faith from within an open Anglican tradition, and although I had encountered the evangelical world at university, and if pressed would have identified with it, I had not fully appreciated quite how zealously the borders were guarded.

In later years Roger Page would become Head of Wholesale at CLC, and UK Director. A good man.

Other shops took a more relaxed approach. The (Roman Catholic) Westminster Cathedral Bookshop was notably broad-minded, cheerfully stocking a range of evangelical authors, a policy continued to this day.

It is a fine line. Christianity, like all religions, is acutely tribal: apart from denominations there are alliances. The evangelical and charismatic wings of the Church of England often have much in common, in worship style and core doctrine, with some strands of the Methodist, Baptist,

Brethren, Newfrontiers, and independent free churches – more, frequently, than with fellow Anglicans. Conversely, the Methodists and Baptists have their liberal wings.

A company such as Hodders, which intentionally catered to all tastes, was in some respects at a disadvantage. In the mid-1970s, the annual Christian Booksellers' Convention was established, and would rapidly become a critically important event for the world of Christian books. At some point in the late 1970s, I was manning the Hodder stand when several evangelical leaders wandered past. As they scanned our offerings, I tried to engage them in conversation, but one of them shook his head. 'You just don't get it,' he informed me. 'What you're publishing. *Who* you're publishing. You're not speaking to us.'

At that time the preferred publisher for much of the evangelical world was Kingsway, a company for which I would later work. Kingsway, whose origins lay with Victory Press, a company specialising in Sunday school prizes, published altogether more trustworthy titles: notably the books of Watchman Nee such as *Sit Walk Stand* and *The Normal Christian Life*. (Nee, who died in 1972, was a Chinese Christian leader who endured harsh persecution.) The evangelical strand of the faith was rapidly gaining the ascendancy in the UK, and many new bookshops were opening with a strongly evangelical identity. The Christian Booksellers' Convention became, *de facto*, a forum for this tradition. This was the era of Billy Graham, and his repeated mantra 'The Bible says . . .' became shorthand for evangelical identity. It was a litmus paper: the Bible says. Who would dare to contradict the Word?

To illustrate the tricky nature of orthodoxy: in 1975 Hodder published the first two books in the I Believe series, edited by Michael Green. Edward had conceived the series after listening to a recording of the famous 'I have a dream' speech by Martin Luther King. The first two volumes were *I Believe in the Holy Spirit* by Green – an instant bestseller – and *I Believe in the Resurrection of Jesus* by George Eldon Ladd. The series, which included contributions from distinguished authors such as David Watson, John Stott, and George Carey (later Archbishop of Canterbury), was intended to include a volume on truth. However, *I Believe in Truth* was scarcely a title to stick in the memory, and the title of the book in the series by Arthur Holmes was ultimately based on a quotation from St Augustine: *I Believe All Truth is God's Truth*.[6]

This penetrated close to the heart of the matter: truth is truth, wherever it is found. Michael Green, a highly respected evangelist and a man of acute intelligence, could just about get away with such a statement. For many in the evangelical world, in practice, the idea that wisdom and insight might abide in other traditions is not readily acknowledged. It is not sufficient for a writer or preacher to be correct. They have to be *sound*.

Michael Green later contributed to the I Believe series a book on Satan, but 'I Believe in Satan' might have given a misleading impression. The exemplary final title, suggested by one of his students, was *I Believe in Satan's Downfall*.

---

6. For those who prefer their theology Reformed, the phrase occurs more than once over the centuries. In his commentary on Titus, John Calvin wrote, 'All truth is from God; and consequently, if wicked men have said anything that is true and just, we ought not to reject it; for it has come from God.'

The noted Anglican evangelist David Watson wrote a string of outstanding volumes for Hodders, including *I Believe in Evangelism* and *I Believe in the Church*. Sales were excellent, but Edward wasn't happy. One morning I looked up to see him pulling books off the shelves beside my desk. 'David Watson's new book is entirely too safe,' he explained, in response to my quizzical look. 'He's not reading widely enough. I'm sending him some heresy.'

In due course the year rolled around, and I was finally given a contract of employment. 'Your face fits,' Edward told me with a smile, handing me a precious envelope. No professor offered tenure could have been more pleased. I was an editor. It said so on my contract.

One morning Edward materialised at my desk and dropped a typescript in front of me. I scanned the title page: *Angels: God's Secret Agents* by Billy Graham.

'Tell me what you think of it,' he enjoined. 'We've been offered British rights.'

Billy Graham was a household name. A series of crusades across the world had given him a degree of influence to rival the Pope. With friends from Horsham Crusader Class, I had attended his 1966 rally at Earl's Court, and had gone forward, very seriously, to renew my commitment.

Mesmerising speaker though he was, Graham's abilities as a writer were modest. After a couple of chapters I began to feel uneasy, and by the end of the book was candidly dismayed. It had little of the precision and research the promising subject demanded, and was dominated by assertions backed by unconvincing anecdotes.

In the book (I quote from Thomas Nelson's Amazon copy)

Dr Graham lifts the veil between the visible and the invisible world to give us an eye-opening account of these behind-the-scenes agents. This best-selling classic records the experiences of Dr Graham and others who are convinced that at moments of special need they have been attended by angels. With keen insight and conviction, Dr Graham affirms that God's invisible hosts are better organised than any of the armies of man—or Satan; angels 'think, feel, will, and display emotions'; angels guide, comfort, and provide for people in the midst of suffering and persecution; at death, the faithful will be ushered by angels into the presence of God.

'With keen conviction': that was the nub of the matter. I had a lot of respect for Billy Graham, whom I later met several times, but he was terribly good at conviction.

Acutely uncomfortable, I knocked on Edward's door, text in hand. Edward looked at my uneasy expression, and nodded. 'Not great, is it?' he commented. 'What do you think we should do?'

I took a deep breath. 'I think we should turn it down,' I blurted.

To my astonishment Edward took me seriously. 'I agree. I'll tell the agent.'

I nodded and returned to my work, thinking little more of the matter.

A week later Edward mooched past my desk, and paused, hands in pockets. 'I've accepted that Graham book,' he told me. 'The agent called me back and begged us to take it.' He grinned. 'I hammered him on the terms, though.'

Sometimes in publishing you have to count before you read. I think Edward had been swayed by some data emerging from the States, because it rapidly became apparent that this was not just another book by an international Christian leader, but a work whose time had come: it was going viral. Billy Graham may not have been a gifted author, but he had an astute understanding of what piqued people's interest, and in choosing this topic he had hit a winner. When we published in hardback a few months later, we sold 40,000 almost overnight.[7]

The following year there followed a host of me-too volumes from other authors and publishers.

It remains an indifferent book, but that is not the whole picture. It touched people's hearts, just as *The Calvary Road* had done. The Holy Spirit doesn't always follow the dictates of the literary.

Eighteen months after I started at Hodders, Jane and I married in Kessingland, in Suffolk, the most easterly village in Britain. Jane's parents hired a huge marquee for the garden. Jane was the eldest of four daughters, the first to marry, and I was an only child, so everyone pulled out the stops. Jane's father, a fisheries scientist, undertook weeks of overtime aboard various trawlers to raise the necessary

---

7. We produced lapel badges promoting the book for use by bookshop staff, but these were not well received: 'Why should we sell Hodders?' was the general response.

cash, braving the high northern seas to measure herring and assess the effectiveness of different nets.

Edward and his wife Gwen attended our wedding: we were delighted they had made the long journey up from Sussex. Edward was very much my boss, but he was also becoming a friend.

4

Increasing Turbulence

Hodder & Stoughton was on the move. For decades the company had occupied premises in St Paul's House, Warwick Lane, in EC4. Close to St Paul's Cathedral, this was the heartland of Britain's publishing industry. Wishing to consolidate publishing and distribution under one roof, and to take advantage of the boom in London's property values, the directors had purchased a site in Dunton Green, near Sevenoaks, in Kent.

Jane and I were pleased. Instead of a train journey, we could both commute by car, for by this point Jane was working for Hodder Educational. The new offices were barely two miles from our little bungalow. In good weather I opted to walk, reading as I went, with one eye out for lamp posts and old ladies.

The move was a huge undertaking. Hundreds of staff had to be relocated, and many more were recruited to replace those who preferred redundancy. New distribution systems had to be set up; an entire cavernous warehouse to be equipped; myriad ancient desks to be replaced. I acquired one such hulking monstrosity. It was beautifully refurbished by Jane's mother, and I kept it for years.

Headaches were endless. Close to the moving date dozens of telephones were installed, the modern units clustered in little groups across the uniform sage carpet (a tint swiftly dubbed 'Dunton Green'). When senior management arrived the following Monday, not one handset was to be seen: thieves had swiped the lot.

A vast glass wall at one end of the warehouse was quickly termed 'the biggest east window this side of Canterbury'.

Interest in the new facility was intense, and I became adept at guiding visitors around the conveyor belts in the warehouse, attempting to distract prelates and visiting American publishers from the naked ladies that populated every supporting pillar. When the Archbishop of Canterbury called in, the horrified warehouse managers, in a belated fit of prudishness, insisted each upright be swathed in brown paper. The Most Revd Donald Coggan, a man of the world, was neither offended nor fooled.

The challenges grew no easier.

'Sales conference in a fortnight, and I want you there,' Edward informed me one morning. 'You'll be presenting the following titles . . .' He handed me a list. 'Work out what you're going to say. Three minutes per book, no more. Now, we've got the after-lunch slot, and everyone's going to be falling asleep. How do you suggest we wake them up?'

Any publisher with a sales team will hold a sales conference, typically two or three times a year, pulling the staff in from around the country and usually putting them up overnight. It's expensive – your main earners are off the road – so it's a focused time. The sales people tend to regard sales conferences as a chance to enjoy themselves, and indeed selling is a demanding job which can erode the soul, so many publishers allow their sales force a degree of latitude. However, the reps are typically a highly critical audience, cynical about the tosh they are being asked to add to their bags, and quick to leap on fluff or incoherence. In this they are encouraged by their managers, who want their subordinates to demonstrate knowledge and skill. It is often a confrontation between editorial and sales, and if things are going badly, it can be a bloodbath. Jobs are on the line.

From the editors' perspective, this is the point where the books over which they have laboured are exposed to public view. They are keen to present book and author in the best possible light, and to report to the writer that the sales team loved it. Editors are accountable: were they right to sponsor this title? Are they out of touch? Is their imagined readership just a chimera? 'Of course there's a market,' an editor will insist, as the sales team roll their eyes.

There is a lot to absorb, with dozens of books to rattle through. Each folder has to be exactly right – woe betide the unfortunate junior who gets a digit wrong in the ISBN – with cover, accurate description, sales points, author bio, and marketing campaign. An adroit editorial director will intersperse the white bread and the sultanas, and keep some blockbuster for the very end.

The following day Edward listened impatiently to my faltering presentation, frequently interrupting. 'Start by reminding them of his previous books. How many did they sell? Well, look them up afterwards. Do you know who he is? No, he was a suffragan but now he's a diocesan bishop, an Anglican shouldn't make that kind of error, get your facts straight. He's got two doctorates. One was in theology, what was the other? He writes articles for the *Observer*, make sure that's in the notes. They need to know he was involved in that controversy last year, but someone was just making mischief: why shouldn't a bishop speak in tongues? It might not help his job prospects, but don't tell them that. Now, he's really an Old Testament specialist, so something on marriage is a bit of a departure for him . . .'

I scribbled away, trying to ask intelligent questions.

An hour later Edward sat back and beamed at me. 'Ok, you'll be fine. Don't let them get to you. It's your first time, they may have some fun. Think of it as a growing experience. So, what *are* you going to do to wake them up?'

How exactly was I going to rouse a group of tough, experienced salesmen who would certainly have enjoyed their lunchtime pints and were viscerally uninterested in religious books?

Overnight Jane and I had talked about this. At university I had dabbled in musicals and theatre, and had recently been handed the young romantic lead in the Hodder & Stoughton Drama Group's production of Sir Arthur Wing Pinero's popular comedy *Trelawny of the Wells*. There was a theatrical costumier not far from the Hodder offices. Edward, to my shock, agreed to my plan.

The sales conference arrived and, taking advantage of the lunch break, Edward and I excused ourselves, repairing to his office to change. Shortly thereafter we made an entrance as His Grace Edward, Cardinal Archbishop of

St Paul's, elegant in his scarlet robes, and his Anglican counterpart the Right Revd Anthony, Bishop of Fleet Street. In the photos Edward, with his customary poise, looks every inch the prelate: his juvenile Anglican sidekick, fashionably long-haired, is clearly an imposter.

I don't remember much of that sales conference, other than to note with relief that the sales folk had been sufficiently diverted by the ecclesiastics in their midst to let me off with some light ribbing.

Subsequent conferences proved far tougher. The reps were not quite the ravaging pack Edward had evoked, but they did know their stuff, they were professionals familiar with Hodder's long output in this sector, and they had no hesitation in pointing out inconsistencies and lacunae. Each treatment had to be sharp, succinct, memorable.

Every publisher hopes to attract household names. At one notable conference, Edward's silver tongue persuaded some genuine celebrities to attend. Held in a smart hotel, the line-up included Malcolm Muggeridge and Cliff Richard. Both men were intensely busy, so a breakfast event was arranged.

Journalist and satirist Malcolm Muggeridge was his usual debonair self. A polished speaker, who had worked in Moscow and Calcutta, Muggeridge had been both deputy editor of the *Telegraph* and editor of *Punch*. A man of elegant wit, with strong and distinctly contrarian views, he had converted to Christianity in his sixties. (In later life he and his wife Kitty would be received into the Catholic Church.) A few years earlier he had published *Something Beautiful for God*, the book which introduced Mother Teresa to readers worldwide. Detractors referred to him as St Mugg.

Sometimes wrong-headed but always entertaining, he had written nearly a score of books. We would be publishing a sharp-tongued reflection titled *Christ and the Media*, in which Muggeridge tartly observed, 'The media in general, and TV in particular, are incomparably the greatest single influence in our society. This influence is, in my opinion, largely exerted irresponsibly, arbitrarily, and without reference to any moral or intellectual, still less spiritual guidelines.' That morning he effortlessly bewitched us, denizens of the media world that we were.

The sales team had been on the razzle the previous night, and – though clean-shaven and smartly dressed – looked distinctly rough, swaying slightly over the eggs and bacon and groping for the coffee. By contrast Cliff Richard, whose autobiography *Which One's Cliff?* would shortly be released, followed a strict regime and arrived at the breakfast buffet cheerful and fresh-faced. After his presentation he had to leave smartly. As his limousine pulled away, one of the team leaned across to Edward. 'Ok,' he muttered, 'I get it. We're publishing Peter Pan.'

Edward decided we needed a religious sales specialist. There was no one in house with an obvious interest in the matter, so we would need to go a-poaching.

Despite the substantial bookshop market, at that time there were few outstanding sales people in the Christian publishing world. The obvious candidate, he quickly decided, was Richard Barnes, then sales manager for IVP UK. Edward trailed some modest adverts in the *Church*

Times and *Church of England Newspaper*. To our satisfaction Richard applied, and was swiftly appointed.

It proved a match not made in heaven. Edward and Richard did not see eye to eye on priorities – Richard focused on organising sales initiatives, while Edward wanted him out on the road, drumming up business. The matter was made more difficult because Richard, as a salesman, came under a different department, and Edward grew steadily more frustrated. I found myself caught between them: Richard and I worked closely together, inevitably, and I appreciated his market knowledge and elegant, man-of-the-world persona. But he and Edward never reached a functional accord.

Looking back, Edward was badly out of order. You have to respect authority structures, but Edward was impatient of such limitations, while Richard's line manager was rightly protective of his staff.

That year saw my first encounter with the complex world of selling rights.

Subsidiary rights (the right to publish a book in translation, or in a different market area in the same language) can command millions. Generally, fiction crosses international boundaries more easily than nonfiction: a good story transcends cultures.

The trade in rights is particularly strong across the Atlantic, but more books flow from America to Britain than vice versa. These days American publishers typically prefer to ship their own stock to UK distributors, rather than releasing rights.

To sell rights, or printed books, from Britain to America is perfectly feasible but less easy, because the US market is relatively insular. However, there is a strong trade from English to other languages, and for some markets (German, Korean, Spanish) the rights can be lucrative. For most translation rights the revenues are modest, but authors prize highly the news of a successful sale of language rights. It is correctly perceived as a genuine tribute that a foreign language publisher should wish to invest, for local benefit, in the expensive process of translating your book.

Accordingly, each year around the world, rights fairs take place – the pre-eminent being, by sheer size and longstanding tradition, the Frankfurt Book Fair. The Frankfurt event is vast, filling a dozen huge multi-storey venues linked by bus, covering everything published worldwide, from maps to falconry, higher mathematics to literary erotica. At the height of the Harry Potter phenomenon, the on-site bus was repainted appropriately and dubbed the 'Hogwarts Express'.

One year I visited Frankfurt when a substantial and expensive volume celebrating the life of the boxer Muhammad Ali had just been released. Truly massive, lavishly illustrated, it was a publishing *tour de force*. There was a showcase at the entrance to the exhibition displaying images from the book, but if you wanted to examine a copy for yourself there was only one option: to wait your turn outside a full-scale boxing ring before climbing through the ropes and *kneeling* in front of the single copy on the canvas floor.

To visit such an event is to plunge into turbulence. Rights executives will meet editors and publishers, each encounter lasting on average not more than thirty minutes, in a flurry of trading, swift thinking, and instant sincerity. It can take months to compile your schedule. Big books are often sewn up off-site before the fair even opens, but there are rich pickings available and every editor dreams of finding an overlooked treasure. The atmosphere is heady and contagious: canny agents may foster a bidding war, and many an overpriced deal has been signed for later repentance.

Such events are focal points for rights agents and agencies, individuals and groups which specialise in creating links between domestic and overseas publishers. Usually these agencies will also act as the liaison between an author and a publisher, negotiating contracts and overseeing payments. When a contract is signed, it will stipulate the territories covered as well as the percentages paid. Agents depend upon the quality of their address books: contacts are everything.

None of which I knew when Winfried Bluth arrived at Hodder's front desk.

Winfried Bluth was at that point – and would remain for years after – one of the most influential Christian literary agents in Europe, possibly the world. As a young soldier he had been captured by the British during World War II, and had spent time in a POW camp. His English was flawless. He was acutely intelligent, and utterly persistent. He travelled incessantly, brokering and dealing.

Edward was out of the office the day Winfried called, almost certainly by design: Winfried was not his favourite person. The receptionist summoned me. Eager to assist the distinguished visitor, I sat down to talk with him about our forthcoming books.

The list included a new title by Mary Wang. Mary was a leader of the Chinese church in exile. At that point the church in China was undergoing harsh repression, as has been sadly true for most of its history, but a flourishing faith movement had developed among the Chinese diaspora in Britain. Mary had previously written *The Chinese Church That Will Not Die*. More accurately, and in the context critically, Edward had interviewed Mary and then written the book for her. Sales had exceeded expectations, and Hodders had sold rights in German and other languages – as Herr Bluth knew perfectly well.

Now Winfried nodded as I mentioned that Mary (i.e. Edward) had completed a sequel.

'I think I could find a German publisher for you,' he smiled, eyes gleaming. 'Would you like me to try?'

I nodded, happy to be able to further the boss's writing career.

The following day I imparted the glad news. There was a brief silence.

'You've just cost Mary and me fifty quid,' observed Edward sourly. 'Winfried will sell the rights for £500, and charge ten per cent agency fee, *plus,*' he took a breath, 'the same percentage for the lifetime of the edition. Our own rights team would have done the job equally well. Next time someone offers to help, ask two questions: why, and how much?'

I had just been handed another life lesson.

In subsequent years I would spend many, many hours in conversation at Frankfurt with editors from a range of language groups. There are flourishing markets for Christian books in many parts of Europe, notably Germany, Scandinavia, and the Netherlands. Margins are tight and print runs often modest, but I have been consistently impressed by the creativity and imagination which flourish in difficult conditions. In the febrile atmosphere of the rights fairs it is easy for integrity to be a victim, but I have had, time and again, the sense that here were people who loved books, and loved the gospel.

One goal of any ambitious Christian publisher will be to publish a version of the Bible. Up to that point Hodder & Stoughton were not known as Bible publishers, a serious weakness for the country's leading religious publishing house. There had been one previous incursion into this complex market: in the early years of the twentieth century, Hodders had published the Moffatt Translation. Dr James Moffatt, a formidable Scottish scholar, had translated the whole, a most considerable undertaking. C.S. Lewis thought highly of Moffatt's work and initially it had proved widely popular. But although it stayed in print, it had not truly won hearts and minds: individual, even idiosyncratic, it featured Moffatt's own preferred sequence of chapters, and was not trusted by the evangelical churches.

To publish a popular Bible is a prize worth the winning. According to the marketing and business site BrandonGaille, 168,000 Bibles are sold every *day* in the

US alone. The Bible is routinely excluded from bestseller lists, as it would always occupy the top spot. The Gideons (an organisation dedicated to giving away copies of the Scriptures) distribute approximately ninety million Bibles a year around the world, in more than a hundred languages. A body started by two commercial travellers in 1908, to date the Gideons have placed over two billion Bibles or portions of the Bible in hotel rooms, schools, hospitals, and other locations[8].

In 1973 – the year before my arrival – Edward had secured British rights to the New Testament of the New International Version, as I mentioned earlier. Of all his immense legacy to Hodder & Stoughton, this is surely the jewel, but it very nearly didn't happen.

The world of Bible publishing is both complex and vast. The work of translation into new languages continues today through agencies such as Biblica (formerly the International Bible Society) and Wycliffe Bible Translators. As the Wycliffe website states, 'The full Bible is now available in close to 700 languages, and the New Testament in over 1,500 languages. But with 1.5 billion people still without access to the full Bible in the language that speaks to them best, our vision of universal access is far from a reality, and the need for translation remains as great as ever.' This huge enterprise has had many consequences, not least the rescuing of many minority languages which might well have dwindled away, their cultures consigned to assimilation and oblivion, had they not been captured in written form as a necessary first step towards Bible translation.

---

8. The UK branch of the Gideons has now been renamed Good News for Everyone.

Despite the size of the potential market, to publish a Bible, in any language, is to take a considerable commercial risk. It's a big investment, without a quick return. The same is true of Bible translation, including into English. The Bible is hugely long, complicated, nuanced, and full of disputed material. Dozens of English versions already exist. Variations in translation can have grave and unpredictable consequences. To add another Bible in English to what was, by the early 1970s, a substantial range of choices, must have seemed a dubious undertaking to Edward's more sceptical and unchurched colleagues.

The Authorised, or King James, Version of the Bible is still widely appreciated, but for all its influence on the English language, it is not easily accessible today. This has prompted a host of alternatives, especially since World War II, and by the time the New International Version arrived on the scene it had a number of well-established competitors, including the Revised Standard Version, 1952; the Jerusalem Bible, 1966; the New English Bible, 1970; the New American Standard Bible, 1971; The Living Bible, 1971; and, dominating the evangelical skyline, the Good News Bible in 1976. It was a crowded marketplace. What could possibly justify another version?

Different translations stem from varying sources, and will reflect both the scholastic and theological emphases of those sources, and the nature of the intended readership. The Revised Standard Version is an updated version of the American Standard Bible, generated by the American National Council of Churches of Christ. The Jerusalem Bible is an English translation of the French Catholic *La Bible de Jérusalem*. The New English Bible (now revised and updated as the Revised English Bible) is a joint (British) venture by Oxford University Press and Cambridge University Press, scholarly and elegant, but not wholly acceptable to evangelical tastes. The Living Bible is a lively paraphrase (not a translation) by the extraordinary Dr Kenneth Taylor, and was widely adopted by many groups such as Youth for Christ: Billy Graham was a particular fan. (Edward had also acquired The Living Bible for Hodders, as we have seen, but for a limited period.) The Good News Bible was developed by the American Bible Society, and like the New English Bible uses the approach of dynamic equivalence (translating thought by thought, rather than word by word). Written in simple everyday language, it is intended for popular use rather than for in-depth study.

Was there really a place for the NIV?

The NIV started life in 1955, as the vision of an engineer from Seattle, Howard Long. Long loved the King James, but sought a reliable, conservative but contemporary version of the Bible which he could share with friends. A dedicated man, he gradually persuaded his denomination, the Christian Reformed Church, and then the National Association of Evangelicals, that such a version was needed.

In 1965 a cross-denominational team of more than a hundred evangelical scholars agreed to start work on a new translation. Notably and importantly, they were a distinctly international group, including participants from America, Canada, England, Australia, and New Zealand. The self-governing Committee on Biblical Translation came into being. Three years later the New York Bible Society came on board as financial sponsor, and in 1973 the New Testament was released.

As the Bible Gateway website summarises the matter:

The Committee held to certain goals for the NIV: that it be an accurate, beautiful, clear, and dignified translation suitable for public and private reading, teaching, preaching, memorising, and liturgical use. The translators were united in their commitment to the authority and infallibility of the Bible as God's Word in written form. They agreed that faithful communication of the meaning of the original writers demands frequent modifications in sentence structure (resulting in a 'thought-for-thought' translation) and constant regard for the contextual meanings of words.

The NIV was bidding for the serious evangelical market.

Edward got wind of the initiative, and took soundings. Initial reactions were discouraging. There were plenty of existing alternatives. To publish would be a huge and expensive undertaking. Edward enquired of friends and contacts at Church House, the administrative centre of the Anglican Church. He talked with those in a position to offer advice at the Baptist Union, the Methodist Conference, the Church of Scotland, even the religious department of the BBC. Seeking a commendation, he approached John Stott, rector of All Souls, London W1, and an authority figure among Anglican evangelicals, but Dr Stott was too busy.

The British Bible Society was entirely focused on the Good News Bible.

A variety of booksellers shook their heads.

Would the Gideons back the new Bible? They were still distributing the Authorised Version. They expressed interest. Their backing was of critical value – but it would be three years before they could make a commitment.

Donald Wiseman, Professor of Assyriology at London University, was one of the translators, and chaired a meeting of the Hodder board. 'I promise you,' he told Edward, 'that within five years the NIV will have a permanent place in the life of many churches.'

It was too big a decision for Edward alone, and he took it to his senior colleagues: Philip and Michael Attenborough, and Eric Major. He shared with them the lacklustre response he had encountered from churches and the book trade. Philip, the chairman, backed the proposal. Eric and Michael agreed.

Edward acquired UK rights. It was a daring move, and it very nearly came unstuck.

Hodders released a British edition of the NIV New Testament in 1973, in a rather unexciting drab blue hardback. The market response was underwhelming. The Good News Bible and The Living Bible were thrilling evangelicals across the country – indeed, across the English-speaking world – and in the UK at least, the NIV was genially ignored. Edward's fellow board members had backed his venture (Edward had a reputation for knowing what he was doing), but I would not have been surprised if muttered voices had questioned whether a discreet withdrawal might be wise.

The New York Bible Society frankly agreed. They were disappointed by the British response, and informed Edward that Hodders would not be granted rights to the full Bible.

Edward was having none of it. In one of the most decisive moves of his life, he flew out to New York, where his assurance, enthusiasm, market knowledge, and personal charisma persuaded the Society to change its mind. He didn't share with me what he said to his fellow directors on his return, but they agreed to support him. It was arguably the boldest and most far-reaching publishing decision he and his colleagues would ever make.

Edward had successfully argued that the British market needed British language and spelling (both true and far-sighted, since this important detail had the effect of keeping out of the UK the subsequent stream of American editions, and keeping control in the hands of H&S). A team of scholars was assembled to undertake the Anglicisation under the leadership of Donald Wiseman (who was, in his spare time, a Crusader leader in the Finchley class, among whose members had been, once, a young Harry Webb, now better known as Cliff Richard).

Hodder & Stoughton was simply unprepared for the scale of the task. The consequences of the Anglicisation clause were profound, because it meant the entire Bible needed to be reset: every verse, every footnote, every superscript numeral. It hugely increased the cost and the time commitment. Hodders had to find, and pay, not only the typesetters and the Anglicisation team but also an army of proofreaders. Bible paper – thin, yet strong and opaque – is a speciality of its own in the world of book production: how to source it? Where would the enormous book be typeset? Who would print it? How would it be marketed? Conventional wisdom was useless. We had to raise our game.

I first began to grasp the scale of the task when Edward summoned me to his home in Crowborough one sunny

Sunday afternoon in high summer. Sitting in his garden, we set to work on the proofs of the Anglicised NIV translation of Genesis, reading verses back and forth to one another, superscript numbers included. After a couple of hours we gave up, cross-eyed with fatigue. We were both meticulous, but the challenge was gargantuan. Any decision we took – for instance, the hyphenation or otherwise of 'no one', a footling choice – might create weeks of work. Thankfully, Edward decided to leave the task to the professionals, and over the months the enormous sets of proofs – first, second, third, sixth – cycled through the office.

In 1977 computer typesetting was just starting to come into widespread use, and as the final versions of the proofs arrived and deadlines loomed, I was sent up to London, weekend after weekend, to work with a technician on what would be the final text for offsetting. Endless sheets of corrected type were extruded for me to check. Every time I found an error, the technician would run off a fresh text, snip it out and stick it with wax over the offending passage. I would approve the correction, and the page would then be photographed.

There were two problems. First, the corrections were not being saved to the master file, an oversight I tried unsuccessfully to explain to Edward, whose grasp of computer technology was even flimsier than mine. Second, the wax sticking the corrections to the original was not that effective, especially in hot weather, and the inevitable happened: a couple of verses in Romans slipped slightly after I had approved them, not sufficiently to render the text incoherent but enough to irritate.

Far-reaching decisions had to be taken: format, binding, balance of hardback to paperback, cover design, cover copy (how do you write a blurb for a Bible?). Print quantities. Prices. Nothing unfamiliar, to a publisher, but on a buttock-clenching scale. An entire marketing campaign had to be devised. The sales team had to be not so much briefed as retrained: selling a Bible requires a whole subset of specialised information and assumptions. The matter was made easier by the enthusiastic support of Richard Barnes, whose kindness and market knowledge had endeared him to the sales staff. He took a keen interest in the new translation and, declaring that he would never market a better product, threw his weight into getting the team up to speed.

Paper was manufactured, the cavernous warehouse near Sevenoaks made ready.

After endless discussions, the board decided on a first printing of 100,000, one of the larger print orders Hodders had placed. Most print runs are guesswork: this was epic gambling. As interest started to snowball the initial quantity rose to 180,000.

The final proofs arrived, and were checked once more.

Just as the first sheets were printed, a critical omission was discovered in Revelation 20:15, which reads, 'Anyone whose name was not found written in the book of life was thrown into the lake of fire.' The 'not' was missing. If the error had not been discovered, the entire print run would have had to be pulped.

Edward masterminded the whole vast, tottering enterprise, and it is a tribute to his abilities that so little went wrong. The rest of the publishing programme had to be kept going, and I left late and arrived early with the rest of the department.

Publication day arrived, with dozens of radio interviews and pieces in the press. Edward handled the brunt of these, but I was given some of the peripherals and instructed severely not to go off-message.

The release of the NIV, remarkably, featured on the 9pm BBC News, and the new complete Bible – much more enthusiastically received than the New Testament – was nailed for months to the top of the bestseller lists.[9] There must have been deep sighs of relief at board level.

'Our first printing should have been 250,000,' observed Jim McEwen, the sales director. 'You should have had more faith!'

Evangelical leaders generally embraced the new translation. The (British) Bible Society, deeply committed to the Good News Bible, was distinctly frosty – an attitude that lasted years – but finally came on board. Within a year or so the Gideons (a distinctly conservative customer) started placing orders.

Edward was delighted. Hodder & Stoughton finally had its own Bible.

Ironically, the valuable property he had struggled so hard to secure was almost certainly a contributing factor in Hodder's ultimate sale to Tim Hely Hutchinson in 1993, creating Hodder Headline, which would be bought by W.H. Smith in 1997, and sold in turn to Hachette Livre in 2005. The NIV has flourished throughout, a blessing to the church, and a lasting commercial asset.

---

9. This was a strange exception to the general rule that bestseller lists exclude Bibles. I have no idea why, but suspect favours were called in.

We quickly grasped that publication was only the start. Zondervan, the American publisher, was churning out edition after edition, and the competitive pressure was strong. On my recommendation Edward interviewed and then appointed Rob Warner, a friend from St Nicholas, Sevenoaks, as Bible co-ordinator. Rob, a graduate in English, had a brilliant mind and was, away from publishing, a captivating preacher. With his arrival our little department increased from three to four, and Rob quickly mastered his brief, grasping fully the importance of getting the software straight and taking the lead in developing new editions of the NIV for popular use.

5

Expanding Horizons

With the success of the NIV Edward was in expansion mode, and declared I needed an assistant of my own. Carolyn Armitage (now Scriven), armed with a degree in English, came recommended by a mutual friend, and would become a firm friend to both Jane and myself, and godmother to our second daughter. I didn't have a clue how to train and direct a subordinate, and Carolyn had to dig into her reserves of patience and diplomacy as I cast about to find jobs for her.

She quickly found her feet, however. Her swift mind and facility with words attracted Edward's attention, and – slightly to her surprise, I think – she found herself recruited to co-author Max Sinclair's *Halfway to Heaven*.

Max Sinclair, a respected young evangelist and Christian leader, with three small children, had been involved in a horrific car accident. His wife Sue, who had been with him in the car, escaped serious injury, but Max had broken his neck and faced lifetime paralysis. With immense courage, bolstered by his faith and the prayers of hundreds of supporters, he made an improbable, though partial, recovery, and was the fourth person in twenty years to walk out of his ward at Stoke Mandeville Hospital, home to the National Spinal Injuries Centre.

To the many who cared about Max and his family, it seemed as if he had returned from the very threshold of the Pearly Gates. Max, an accountant, was a fluent public speaker, but in his long convalescence was not up to the sustained effort of writing a book. Carolyn's sympathetic and engaging account of his experiences captured the public imagination, and for years afterwards Max was in great demand as a speaker. A few years later, he founded Christian Viewpoint for Men.[10]

Carolyn's job was not at all easy. To be a ghost-writer you have to interview your subject, sometimes over months; wrestle an unwieldy mass of detail into coherence; create an absorbing narrative or argument; master your subject's idiom without losing your own sense of style; avoid the pitfalls of irrelevance and inaccuracy; steer your subject away from pet peeves and libellous asides. Co-authors are a vital component in the publishing world. Many public figures depend on them. Good co-authors are hard to find, and should be cherished. I have had the very good fortune to work with two or three highly capable co-authors, and have pushed hard for them to receive a decent share of the royalties.

Inspired – perhaps provoked – by Carolyn's endeavours, I set to work myself.

The first literary endeavour Jane and I undertook was not a piece of co-authoring, but a translation. Richard

---

10. Now Christian Vision for Men, it has 500 groups around the UK with overseas offices in North and South America, Africa and Asia.

Wurmbrand (see pp 19, 23) had given Edward a copy of a book by one of his wife Sabrina's fellow prisoners, Nicole Valéry. Entitled *Bénie Sois-tu Prison* (literally, 'Bless You, Prison'), it was a stirring tale of suffering, endurance, faith, and integrity under the oppressive regime of Romania's Nicolae Ceaușescu, whose brutal dictatorship would last more than twenty years. Edward handed me the paperback, which I read with interest, and with Edward's approval I asked Pastor Wurmbrand if he would like it translated. He gladly accepted the suggestion, agreed the fee we suggested, and for a year Jane and I hammered out a page or two each morning before leaving for work. Hodders subsequently released it under the title *Prisoner Rejoice*.

Meanwhile, I continued to learn from experience.

Joni was released by Zondervan in 1976. Joni (pronounced Johnny) Eareckson, an active teenager, had misjudged the depth of water while diving and broken her neck. The resulting quadriplegia had caused her to question her faith, and to wrestle with depression and thoughts of suicide. As part of her occupational therapy, she had been invited to try painting with a brush clamped in her teeth: her art, widely admired, had given her a new grip on life. Her first book *Joni*, subtitled *The unforgettable story of a young woman's struggle against quadriplegia and depression,* proved a bestseller.

British rights were available, and I took home a copy to read. I think if Edward had seen it, he would have leapt at the opportunity, but unfortunately it reached my desk first – I had become the primary filter for new proposals.

The story failed to grip. At that time Joni was entirely unfamiliar to British readers. Unaware of the furore surrounding the American edition, I found the account rather depressing, American in focus, a little saccharine, and foolishly took no action.

Weeks later I heard about the runaway success across the water, and took another look, but by that point Pickering & Inglis had acquired rights. I called the director of P&I and suggested a joint edition, but nothing doing. I had missed a truly major success. Joni has now written more than forty books, carved out a ministry as a speaker, and is justly revered for her courage and gracious demeanour.

Edward commented cheerfully that you were not a publisher until you had turned down your first bestseller. I knew better: it was a criminal failure of imagination on my part not to see the value of the story. I had flinched from the heart-wrenching narrative; I had overlooked Joni's indomitable spirit; I had failed to perceive that others might react differently.

This was the truth I learned, and of which I was subsequently reminded every time I passed a church bookstall: the publisher cannot publish simply for her- or himself. It takes experience, and humanity, and rigorous humility, to see beyond your own boundaries. You need to know how people think, and to remember that your reactions may not be theirs. A fair percentage of my subsequent errors have sprung from the occasions when I have lost sight of this.

Close on the heels of the *Joni* episode came two books which were altogether serendipitous. The first was *Man from a Far Country*.

Karol Józef Wojtyła was elected Pope in 1978, taking the name John Paul II. A man of immense character and ability, he was the first Polish Pope, provocatively chosen at a time when the atheistic Soviet Union still had most of Eastern Europe firmly in its grip. The Catholic Church welcomed the new Pope as a breath of fresh air (possibly erroneously, as he was highly conservative, though his charisma was undeniable). The wider world embraced him wholeheartedly.

Edward and I were not students of the Vatican, but this was a golden opportunity. I suggested we contact Mary Craig, a Catholic laywoman, journalist, and reputedly one of the brains setting questions for the series *Mastermind*. She had previously written a biography of the controversial Catholic peer Lord Longford. Mary accepted the commission, and within weeks we rushed out *Man from a Far Country*, a quick but coherent portrait of the new Pope. We were first to market, and the initial printing of 20,000 was snapped up in days.

No credit where no credit is due. Many years later, at Lion Hudson, on the election of Pope Benedict XVI, I persuaded our managing director, Paul Clifford, to rush out another swift papal biography. It failed. Josef Ratzinger was not Karol Wojtyła. Formulae rarely apply in publishing.

The second unexpected success was linked to David Watson, vicar of St Michael-le-Belfrey, York, a noted evangelist and pioneer of the charismatic renewal in the Church of England. In support of one of David's book launches Edward sent me up to York, where I sat eating cake and drinking tea around the vicarage's kitchen table with a group of young actors including Murray Watts, Paul Burbridge, and Nigel Forde, founding members of the Riding Lights Theatre Company.

Riding Lights was at that point newly formed, and rising sharply in popularity. The members of the team were ebullient, cheerful, witty, and in great demand for their polished quick-fire routines based on biblical stories. 'The Parable of the Good Punk Rocker' was a particular favourite. They would shortly embark on the first of a series of immensely popular national tours.

Within a few weeks of our meeting, Murray and Paul sent me a collection of about twenty brief but penetrating drama scripts, in the hope they might make a book. At that point there was no discernible demand for such a volume: the category of 'church resources' was limited mainly to liturgical materials and books of prayer.

This was something new. I loved the crackling energy, imaginative leaps, and absurd word plays. Edward and the sales team were entirely dubious. Nevertheless, David Watson was willing to contribute a foreword, so Edward consented. In 1979 Hodder released *Time to Act: Sketches and Guidelines for Biblical Drama*. Within a couple of years, over 100,000 copies had been sold and every youth group in the country seemed to have discovered the joy of acting.

We had, inadvertently, backed a winner. The churches, like the rest of the population attuned to intelligent silliness by Monty Python, loved the Watts/Burbridge blend of surreal comedy and spiritual content.

A lot of publishing is about staying awake. Edward had acquired Richard Wurmbrand's *Tortured for Christ* – an account of the Romanian pastor's fourteen years in prison for his faith – simply because he had been at a meeting where the poor man had spoken shortly after his release (Wurmbrand had been ransomed to the West for a price of $10,000). Other publishers, Edward reminisced, had been part of the meeting, but only Edward had made the approach.[11]

At this point Colin Urquhart and his wife Caroline came into our lives once more. How do you follow such a ground-breaking volume as *When the Spirit Comes*? The door was wide open to anything Colin might propose.

He decided to write a novel. *My Father is the Gardener* is a fictional account of renewal coming to an Anglican parish, and packs an impressive punch for those with an ear to hear. However, Colin's skills as a novelist did not entirely match his wisdom as a man of God. Jane and I were eager to expand our portfolio as writers and editors, and offered to go through the text, smoothing out dialogue and tightening up characterisation. The book did remarkably well, and copies are still in demand.

Jane and Caroline struck up a rapport. It is not easy being the partner of someone powerfully used by God, and Caroline reported to Jane that sometimes Colin would return home from a meeting positively glowing: not in the sense of the conventional metaphor, but actually, genuinely shining with the light of the Spirit. It didn't make their relationship any easier: how can you accept the loving touch of a man whose hands have, under the power of the Spirit, performed miracles of healing?

When Edward suggested to Caroline that she too might write a book, Jane was the obvious choice as co-author. *His*

---

11. Wurmbrand, a charismatic, uncompromising evangelist and preacher, who in his youth had been a Communist agent, would go on to write at least eighteen books, of which the best known are *Tortured for Christ* and *In God's Underground*. He founded the body that would become Voice of the Martyrs, an international organisation defending the rights of persecuted Christians.

God, My God was published in 1983: Jane's first book, and a good one.

By this point I had worked at Hodders, and for Edward, for five years, and was growing restless. One day I spotted an advert in the *Church of England Newspaper*: Scripture Union were recruiting for a publishing manager. It was a great job, and a step up. With some trepidation I showed the ad to Edward. He had been an uncompromising boss, tough-minded and rigorous, but he could be generous, and he encouraged me to pick up the phone.

SU's interviewers were gracious and positive, and something of the glitter of the Hodder reputation must have followed me, for a day or two later they offered me the job.

Which I turned down.

At the time the Hodder list had a touch of gold about it, and I found I simply couldn't walk away from so many great books. At least, that was the reason I offered.

I have made many bad choices, but this is one of the decisions I most profoundly regret. It was extremely annoying to Scripture Union, who had to restart their search. From my point of view, as assessed over the following weeks, it smacked uncomfortably of small-minded conservatism. If I had taken up the post at SU, I would have joined a bright, creative, and ambitious team, whose Sound and Vision unit was breaking all kinds of new ground (their number included the hugely talented James Jones, later Bishop of Liverpool). Who knows what might have developed?

That day I miscalculated, badly.

Edward accepted my decision to stay, but I think he was disappointed in me. A few years later he would write in his memoir *An Unfading Vision*[12] of the importance of taking risks, quoting Paul Tournier's *The Adventure of Living*: 'The Bible is the book of adventure and must be read as such. Not only the adventure of the world and of humanity, but the personal adventure of each man and woman whom God touches, calls, and sends into action.' Edward himself, after reading Tournier, had stepped out of the rut in which he perceived himself to be – ironically, leaving Scripture Union for Hodder & Stoughton. Faced with the same decision, I had flunked it.

Looking back, I think I had been brought up with the post-World War I mindset, formed in the Depression era, when if you were so lucky as to have a job, you clung to it white-knuckled, inching upwards through the ranks while your hair receded and your waist expanded, until the time came for the carriage clock and the bungalow by the sea. My parents had both stuck with the same teaching jobs (in my father's case a role he cordially disliked, though he was a popular master) for decades.

In subsequent years I would take Tournier's admonitions, as channelled by Edward, very much to heart, and would find within myself a capacity for risk-taking that would disconcert my careful mother. My father's appetite for adventure, I think, had been sated by World War II, during which he was a liaison officer between the French and British forces in the Middle East. The man I remember yearned for a quiet life. Yet in him, too, a restless spirit

---

12. London: Hodder & Stoughton, 1982

lurked: when I was a teenager he applied for a game warden's position in Scotland, a post which would have meant a profound upheaval for us all. He didn't get the job.

There's a theological aspect to this. It depends where your security lies. If you march to a beat measured out by the respect of your peers, or the solidity of your bank balance, then you probably shouldn't go into publishing, which is really a form of legal gambling. You especially – and this has grown more true with the passing years – should not become a Christian publisher, where the risks are incessant and the margins mostly derisory. But if your security is in Christ; if you are part of a church which hearkens to the voice of the Spirit; if the coin you desire cannot be counted, but may be measured in lives touched and transformed: then to publish well can be a source of blessing, both to you and to those whose minds and spirits are stirred.

As I reflected over the next several months, I realised the restlessness in my spirit had not diminished. Had I been mesmerised by Hodder & Stoughton, and by Edward? Was I simply coming to terms with the fact that books may have wings, but publishers plod?

Jane had recently given birth to our first daughter, Abigail, and her arrival prompted us to ask questions about the future. What did God have in mind for us? Were we being prompted towards a bigger adventure? We were deeply involved in the work amongst teenagers and young adults at the thriving church of St Nicholas, Sevenoaks. The young adults' group, Network, met each Sunday evening in our home, and regularly attracted more than twenty people.

I began to wonder whether the Scripture Union experience was just a springboard for something more. I had failed to grasp one opportunity for adventure; might there be something bigger?

Jane commented that life with me was like living at a crossroads, as I debated the best way forward.

Finally, with her support, I started the process of testing whether I had a vocation to become an Anglican priest. We were sent on an exploratory weekend, then invited for an interview with the Diocesan Director of Ordinands.

Was this moment something of God? We stepped warily into the DDO's comfortable study, booklined and warm, wondering whether this was the watershed we had been sensing.

The gentleman was genial, but his words were chilling. 'I think it is possible you have a vocation,' he began carefully, 'but you can't pursue it from your current church.' He paused, looking at our puzzled faces. 'I don't know if you realise, but your minister doesn't support your candidacy. He doesn't approve of your charismatic ideas.'

This was a shock. The Revd Ken Prior, rector of St Nicholas, Sevenoaks, was an old-school evangelical. There was at that time, right across America and Western Europe, a profound division between evangelicals and charismatics. It boiled down to a question of authority: evangelicals emphasised the primacy of the Bible, while charismatics called attention to the power of the Holy Spirit. Charismatics viewed evangelicals as hampered by dogma; evangelicals regarded charismatics as emotional hotheads. Feelings ran strongly on both sides. I had edited several texts on aspects of the charismatic renewal by authors such as David Watson, Michael Green, and Michael Harper (all priests in the Church of England, incidentally, though Michael Harper would later join the Russian Orthodox). How could you read a book such as Harper's *Let My People Grow!* and not feel excited? I and other younger members of our church had been entranced by the possibilities: the Holy Spirit was moving in the land. We had made little secret of our views, and Ken Prior saw fit to reprove me after an evening service for the error of my ways, bellowing (there was no other word for it) at me in the middle of the church that 'I will have none of your charismatic rubbish'.

To be fair, I had certainly been intemperate in something I had said: I had been deeply impacted by the possibility that God might speak and act today, that miracles and healing might still take place. I cannot remember what had irked Ken so badly, but I had certainly managed to provoke him.

Now the DDO looked at us with compassion, but explained that we needed a sponsoring church. If our rector was not in favour, we would need to move to a new congregation and spend several years winning their trust and support before the matter could reasonably be reviewed.

I suspect, now, that if the call to ordained ministry had been deeply rooted, we might have taken the decision to move. But it felt as if the door had been slammed. Which way should we turn?

Then, entirely unexpectedly, Edward announced he was getting married again.

Edward's professional life was breath-taking; his private life was turbulent. His first marriage, to Gwen, a concert pianist, had ended with her early and untimely death from lung cancer (a painful irony, because she had never smoked). He was devastated by her passing. He returned to work far too early, white around the eyes, barely coherent and hardly able to focus: I remember him struggling to recall how to write a cheque. 'The firm became a substitute for home,' he wrote in *An Unfading Vision*. For a year or more he mourned, and Jane and I offered him such companionship and comfort as two youngsters could manage.

But he needed an outlet for his immense reserves of energy. As he started to recover, his restless spirit lighted upon an adventure, and he booked himself a ticket on the Trans-Siberian Express, flying to the remote city of Khabarovsk, a few miles from the Chinese border, and travelling back nearly 1,400 miles to Irkutsk. During the decades of Soviet rule, repression of Christians was fierce, and a manuscript called *Three Generations of Suffering* had been smuggled out to the West, where I had the privilege of editing it. Its author, Georgi Vins, was still held in a Siberian labour camp, the third generation of his family to be imprisoned for Christ. Edward wanted to see for himself the land and people among whom Vins was incarcerated. 'It was unlikely I would be able to visit him in his camp,' Edward wrote, but he came closer than he had intended when the car he and three companions had chartered for an excursion into the *taiga* took a wrong turning and they found themselves at the back gate of a labour camp, one of many scattered through the intense remote cold of the Siberian wilderness.

He was not called to a solitary life. One day he called me into his office, handed me £20 and asked me to buy flowers and perfume. To my questioning eyebrow he explained that he was taking a lady to dinner. I gleefully drove into Sevenoaks and acquired a dozen red roses and a bottle of Chanel No 5. I later learned that his dinner guest, Ann, had received the gifts with appreciation: such things were not part of a missionary's life.

Ann – Dr Ann Varcoe – had been a friend of Gwen, Edward's first wife. A gynaecologist, immensely skilled and very highly qualified, she had worked for some years with the Overseas Missionary Fellowship in Thailand. Returning to the UK to look after her ageing mother, she was taken aback by Edward's invitation; taken aback still more when after a few meetings – Edward was not the world's most patient suitor – he asked her to be his wife. Slightly stunned, she accepted. During years of tight budgets and tighter schedules, daily emergencies piled upon nightly crises, and all the frictions attendant upon ex-pat living, Ann had not included marriage among her life plans. Now she found herself a bride to one of Britain's most formidable publishers.

She rose to the challenge with humour and dignity, helped by a ready wit, immense reserves of kindness, and the intelligence that allowed her, as Edward admitted ruefully a few months later, to complete the *Times* crossword while beating him at Scrabble.

The course of true romance did not run smooth. Edward and I had lunch together one day. Over coffee he shook his head. 'I had an attack of the jitters last week,' he said. 'I rang Ann to tell her I couldn't marry her.' I stared at him, my spoon frozen in mid-air. He added a dash of milk, and looked up. 'She told me, "Just take no notice. I came to the same conclusion last month. It'll pass."'

Within a year of their dinner date, Jane and I were pleased to attend their wedding, conducted by David Pawson, pastor of the Millmead Centre in Guildford – and, of course, a Hodder author.

Edward and Ann would have many years together. Their life experience and temperaments were not obviously compatible: Edward was a mercurial, opinionated Yorkshireman, something of a bruiser; Ann a quiet but determined lady whose family hailed from Cornwall. Yet they had found love, and each respected the other. They were, rather against the odds, immensely happy.

A few months after their wedding, Edward announced he was quitting his job. He hadn't had a better offer, but felt it was time to move. His personal life was secure, the NIV was landed and established, Hodder Christian Books were in fine shape: he wanted new mountains to climb. True to his inspiration, Paul Tournier, he felt it was time for a new adventure.

His fellow board members were horrified, rightly suspecting Rob Warner and I were not capable of stepping into his shoes. Edward received representations from his colleagues, offering him anything he wanted – his own separate offices, more staff, hot and cold running cherubs. But Edward was adamant: he wanted to strike out on his own, and within weeks he had gone.

His first move was to offer to buy thousands of books from the Hodder warehouse at a basement price. Managing director Eric Major, to whom Rob and I now reported, gladly accepted the deal: Edward immediately sold the overstocks to shops around the country. Rob and I looked at each other. Why couldn't we have done that?

He then set up Edward England Books, effectively the only religious literary agency in the country, and authors came flocking. As Rob and I struggled to develop our publishing programme, we discovered time and again that our contacts were actually Edward's contacts, and our offers to authors had to take into account that we were now bidding against other publishers – Collins, Marshalls, Kingsway, Mowbrays, IVP, SPCK. Edward's personal prestige had sheltered us to some degree from the cold commercial winds, but that shelter was gone. Rob and I had to build up our own range of connections, or become irrelevant.[13]

The Hodder religious department was quickly subsumed as Eric Major moved swiftly to bring the profitable list under his thumb. The move to Sevenoaks had not pleased the general market editors and directors, who wanted to stay in easy lunching distance of their London networks, and soon after the new HQ had been set up, the capital's pull proved too strong and Hodders leased space in Bedford Square. Within months Rob and I were ousted

---

13. Early on Rob and I conceived of a series we thought Michael Green might edit, and invited Michael down to Dunton Green. I met him at Sevenoaks station. We drew up outside our HQ so he could fetch his bag from the back of the car. Incautiously I slammed the tailgate shut, smiting Michael on the crown of his head, and the poor man reeled away, clutching his scalp. He was very good about the incident, but inflicting bodily harm on your authors is not recommended. The series never materialised.

from operations in Kent and relocated to an eyrie in that august publishing district.

Rob was appointed senior editor; I became managing editor. The Christian books operation consisted of the two of us, so the labels were meaningless. Carolyn was transferred to the marketing department. Eric Major was a fair-minded but deeply competitive man (he had been an Olympic-grade sprinter in his youth), and a committed Catholic, but nowhere near the wavelength of the evangelical world where most of our books were selling. The move to London brought new tensions as we evaluated and were appraised by the marketing team, who had also relocated. Edward's authority had eased the acceptance of many books, but now every decision we proposed was stringently reviewed and often overturned.

This came to a head, for me, when I made another inexcusable error.

We had published, with marked and unanticipated success, Richard Foster's ground-breaking *Celebration of Discipline*. Edward had bought British rights, and we published with minimum effort and expense, simply using the American setting – far too cramped for the small paperback format we chose – and giving the volume an unappealing, drab green cover. Yet the book triumphed. Foster, a Quaker, had introduced to a wider audience the patterns of spiritual discipline which for centuries had undergirded the life of serious Catholics, but which had been ignored or mislaid, particularly by evangelical churches. The book spoke of the inward disciplines of meditation, prayer, fasting, and study; the outward disciplines of simplicity, solitude, submission, and service;

and the corporate disciplines of confession, worship, guidance, and celebration. The book offered obvious truth and wisdom, and an insight into a worldview I, for one, was lacking.

The American edition had been published by Harper & Row. When their rights department wrote offering UK rights for Foster's forthcoming sequel *Freedom of Simplicity* I was elated: Foster was sheer gold, and the decision was obvious. When I passed Eric that morning in the corridor, I chirpily mentioned the new proposal, but to my surprise he frowned, cautioning me against precipitate action. I would not have been able to offer a contract on my own recognisance, of course, but Eric's lack of enthusiasm made me pause, doubting my own judgement, and it was several weeks before I brought the matter to the relevant meeting. I was authorised to make an offer, but when I did so I was too late: an enterprising editor at SPCK had got wind of the book, and jumped in first. *Freedom of Simplicity* would be published to great acclaim – but not by Hodders.

I was appalled: the failure still rankles, decades later. When Richard Barnes discovered we were not to publish Foster's second book, he quizzed me in detail, wanting to know how such a prize had escaped our grip. I temporised, unwilling to admit a passing comment had so floored me.

Why had Eric reacted so negatively? I am not sure: he may simply have been insufficiently aware of the reception for *Celebration of Discipline*. What bothered me more, and bothers me still, is that I should have been so easily daunted, to have paid such attention to a passing comment by a distracted and over-busy chief executive.

I should have had the confidence to pursue what I knew to be sound.

It was a frustrating time. Within a couple of years both Rob and I would be gone: Rob to study for ordained ministry in Oxford, and then enjoy a distinguished academic career, ultimately as Vice-Chancellor of Plymouth Marjon University.

I, meanwhile, set out to become a missionary publisher.

6

Intermission: All Nations

One evening in 1980, at a church service in Sevenoaks, I found myself sitting next to Peter Cunliffe.

Peter and his wife Bobbie were American missionaries. Peter was the CEO of Mundo Cristão – Christian World Publishers – based in São Paulo, Brazil. A gracious, focused man, Peter was also suffering from flu, which was not improving his holiday in England. His hosts had urged him to stay in bed, but he had felt compelled to show up.

Peter was that most unusual of beings, a missionary with a specific calling to rescue struggling publishers. Sponsored by American friends and churches, he had spent over a decade learning Portuguese and sorting out the financial troubles of Mundo Cristão. A commissioning editor, a visionary, and a highly numerate executive, he could have held down a senior position anywhere in the publishing world. Like so many missionaries, he eschewed comfort and the trappings of success to build up a ministry. Today, long after his departure, Mundo Cristão is flourishing.

As Jane and I sat and chatted with Peter and Bobbie, we began to wonder if there might be something of the divine about this meeting. Peter had spent many years building up Mundo Cristão, urging it onto a firm financial footing, to the point where it was one of the strongest Portuguese-language Christian publishers. At that point it – like many publishers in developing nations – was heavily dependent on translations from North American writers, but he was determined to find and establish Brazilian authors.

'That's really a job for my successor,' he wheezed, 'because I want to hand the company over. As soon as I've found a replacement, I'm off to Paris. A publisher there needs some help.'

Did he speak French?

'Not yet, but I'm learning.'

Jane and I looked at each other.

'So,' I ventured, 'you need someone to run Mundo Cristão.' A pause. 'What qualifications would they need?'

Over the next few days our friendship began to develop, continuing by post after Peter and Bobbie returned to Brazil. In retrospect, the outcome of what became an extended interview was obvious: our faces fitted. Jane had long been fired up by the idea of going to South America as a missionary. I had trained as a publisher – indeed, had been apprenticed, though the term was never used, under a master of the craft. Both Jane and I had studied French; learning Portuguese, another Latin language, would be a pleasure.

But how would we go? Peter was funded privately by a group of friends, a financial model common in the States. This is not the pattern for most British missionaries, who are generally sponsored through mission agencies. For us this meant SAMS, the South American Missionary Society, originally founded as the Patagonian Mission in 1844 by Captain Allen Gardiner of the Royal Navy.

A dogged, capable, and enterprising man, Gardiner and six companions starved to death in 1851, weeks before supplies arrived, while attempting to establish a mission to the local Indians in the inhospitable wastes of Tierra del Fuego. When news reached Britain, the men were seen as martyrs. Their deaths seized public imagination and funds poured in, sufficient to build and equip a suitable vessel for use as a base. In 1860, the Captain's son, Allen Gardiner Jr, established a second mission station in Chile. As the work grew, the mission was christened the South American Missionary Society. Today the Anglican Church in Latin America is a vigorous descendant.

Up to this point I had had little contact with the world of missions, but what had I been missing? This was heady stuff.

Now SAMS seemed the most likely avenue to help us, so we knocked on their door. Would they sponsor us to join Mundo Cristão? With caveats – a story told elsewhere[14] – they agreed to accept our candidacy.

Not, however, without training.

Canon Philip King, General Secretary of SAMS, was a kindly, rather patrician gentleman, and he twisted himself in knots as he delivered the outcome of tests, probing questionnaires and days of interviews. In their view, he told us, Jane had a genuine vocation, but – he squirmed with embarrassment – they weren't sure about me. I listened

---

14. *Taking My God for a Walk*, Tony Collins. Oxford: Monarch Books, 2016, pp22ff

to his slightly flustered explanation. 'So,' I summarised, 'SAMS will review the matter once I have given up my job and done a year's training?'

In other words, was I serious? Their challenge fell somewhere between a fleece and a hurdle.

Peter Cunliffe was not pleased with the proposed delay, but there was no avoiding the matter if we wanted SAMS to back us.

Several colleges existed where we might train, and on Philip King's advice we approached two: Trinity College, Bristol, and All Nations Christian College in Ware. Trinity interviewed us first, and to my dismay I found myself being quizzed by Gervais Angel, a senior member of the faculty whose book I had turned down only weeks before. In due course – he was more gracious than I – an offer arrived, but only for myself: Trinity was an Anglican establishment, geared to training vicars. Jane might follow some classes, if she wished.

All Nations was altogether more realistic about the challenges facing a couple on the mission field, taking the view that married couples *had* to train together, and providing good crèche facilities to back their conviction, as well as a live link to a room adjacent to the main lecture hall where mothers might feed their babies while keeping up with their notes.

When the offer from All Nations arrived, we were overjoyed: there was a plan; we had a purpose; in our future lay Brazil.

With little to-do, we sold our house, buying a smaller residence in Ware. Eric Major bought me lunch and bade me farewell. Carolyn Armitage took over my desk and responsibilities, rising brilliantly to the challenge. Our rector, Ken Prior – who had so firmly blocked my thoughts of ordination – was conversely delighted to have a pair of missionaries sent out by his church, and to our enduring appreciation, St Nick's not only helped to finance our training, but prayed regularly for us for years afterwards.

That summer was an odd intermission. Jane was expecting our second child, and her first pregnancy had been difficult. For weeks prior to the birth we lived with her parents in Suffolk. Eric Major, keen to move things along, had offered me several months' salary on the understanding that I would leave promptly. I was at a loose end, and filled the time by writing a book for George Verwer.

George Verwer is one of the most extraordinary missionaries I have ever met. A thin, intense American fireball, he has the gifts of evangelism and leadership, and has inspired thousands of young men and women to give their lives to Christian service. Founder of the agency Operation Mobilisation (spelt with an 's' because he was based in Britain and wanted it to sound British), he is one of the fathers of modern Christian mission. He commands widespread loyalty and love, and has an infectious enthusiasm for Christian books, of which he has purchased and given away tens of thousands over the years.

I had offered to work with him on a book, and in return he sent me a box of cassette tapes from his many talks.

They were not quite what they seemed, because George was much given to digression. A tape labelled 'Tithing' could turn out to be mostly about intercessory prayer. One labelled 'Mission in a secular age' might prove to focus mainly on sexual fulfilment in marriage. In the end,

I took a pair of scissors to my careful transcript and created a book from the collage, cutting and pasting passages which might reasonably relate one to another and tying the ends together. The result, *No Turning Back* (a felicitous title suggested by Rob Warner), was a book on Christian discipleship.

Quite unexpectedly, the book (released by Hodders in the summer of 1983, simultaneously with Jane's – and Caroline Urquhart's – *His God, My God*) performed astonishingly well, entirely through George's reputation: I had hitched my wagon to his star. It would sell at least 200,000 copies in English and be translated into over twenty languages. For more than a decade my share of the royalties would pay for our family holidays.

I completed the task days before Jane went into labour. Our new-born daughter Carrie in our arms, we set off to become missionaries too.

All Nations was a revelation, catering as it did for students from many different backgrounds. Years of editing Christian books had given me a smattering of theology, but now it felt as if the riches of the Orient were laid out for our pleasure. Christology, missions theory and history, church development, the structure of the Bible, essentials of counselling, New Testament Greek: the courses were a delight. Because many of the students would be working far from medical and technical resources, we were invited to follow modules in primary health care, hairdressing, emergency dentistry, and the basics of motor mechanics. Any married man was expected to learn the rudiments of field midwifery (I had attended the birth of both our daughters, so had a head start on some of my green-gilled companions as we watched detailed explanatory videos).

We loved it. We were learning so much that St Nick's sponsored us for a second year. With good grace Peter accepted our decision, though he made it clear we needed to start language studies urgently.

We were just making plans to do so when our world imploded.

Our first daughter Abigail had been slow to speak, slow to walk, and a series of investigations by paediatricians confirmed what we had started to fear: her development was awry. Carrie was a robust and cheerful child, but Abbie was indefinably fragile, mentally and physically. As our second year at All Nations ended, we were told, unambiguously, that her only chance of acquiring adequate speech – at the age of four she had few recognisable words – was to stay in an English-speaking context.

With a most heavy heart we informed Peter Cunliffe, and our contacts at SAMS, that we could not come to Brazil. The friends we had made at college dispersed to the winds. Peter Cunliffe started restructuring his plans: he understood what we were facing, but it was a blow to him too. We suddenly found ourselves marooned in a Hertfordshire town, without networks, without a job, without a future, without a point. We were devastated. In our early thirties, and effectively unnecessary. Whatever was God playing at?

It was a tough time. Yet All Nations formed my future as a publisher. It taught me a great deal about my faith, the Bible, Christian doctrine, and the spiritual life. Crucially, the years of study in the history of missions opened my eyes to the part the missionary enterprise had played in the development, not just of the Church, but of the world. Christian missionaries had introduced health care and education right around the globe, and by their efforts in Bible translation had rescued hundreds of languages from extinction and prevented cultures fading into history. Mission stories are studded with people of extraordinary tenacity and character.

The world of missions, at that point, was the embarrassing poor relation of the Western Church, too easily (and too glibly) associated with the echoes of Empire. Hardly anyone was publishing books on the subject. It was a neglected topic, and a neglected marketplace: an opportunity.

7

MARC Europe

In 1983 we left All Nations, and found ourselves without a future. Everything had been geared to one end. We had stood apart from the commercial world. Over the previous two years we had bought few clothes, indeed little other than toiletries and books. Our weekly routine had been dominated by lectures and student life. Now we had graduated.

Not all was grim. We had a little house in Ware, which we owned outright; we had a beaten-up ancient Morris Marina (also owned outright). But we had spent two years learning skills which the British marketplace might choose to ignore. We needed to think about schools for the girls. Our college friends had vanished with the ending of the academic year. And we didn't know what we were *for*.

I signed on for unemployment benefit. Each week I would go down to the job centre and register myself for work, and receive the welcome but demeaning state support to which I was entitled by accident of birth. In the end I was on the dole for less than two months, but it was an unsettling period in which to come to terms with my own marginal value.

Those weeks, coming as they did hard on the heels of Abbie's diagnosis, forced upon me a profound reappraisal. I had worked, very hard, to succeed. Apart from failing my first driving test[15] and failing to get into Cambridge, things had gone well. A combination of graft, judiciously chosen parents, and the right accent had brought me modest academic success, a decent job, and some measure of wealth and security.

Now our beautiful elder daughter faced a difficult future. Our friends, with whom we had laughed and wept, were gone. Our families were miles away. God seemed to have quit too. And I was, for the first time in my life, redundant.

Jane coped well, better than me. The girls demanded much of our time, but when she was not running after them, she would assist me in looking through the 'wanted' sections of various magazines and newspapers, and attempt to bolster my flagging spirits. I remember pounding my fist on the floor in fury and pain one afternoon and shouting, 'I know I am worth something!' She had a lot to put up with.

My obvious – indeed my only obvious – course of action was to return to the world of publishing. I applied to Kingsway, but was turned down: they didn't need another editor. I applied to Lion, and they invited me for an interview, but I wasn't offering what they needed, and again was turned away. I looked back ruefully to the point, several years previously, when Scripture Union had offered me a good job, and I had refused. What had I been thinking?

---

15. I have taken four driving tests, and passed three, one of life's more pleasing statistics.

At that very miserable moment a card arrived from Edward England, encouraging me and adding, 'In the economy of heaven nothing is wasted.' It was an encounter with profound truth.

Since that time I have, on three occasions, and very reluctantly, had to make people redundant, and have watched decent men and women face the fact that their services were no longer required: *they* were no longer required. When I have handed people their papers, I have tried to do so with compassion. I have walked in their shoes.

In later years I would work for both Kingsway and Lion.

Possessions may weigh you down, but life on the margins is not fun.

As students we had existed, in many respects, free from money worries. Friends and grant-making trusts had supplemented the valuable income from St Nicks, meaning that we could buckle the two ends of the month. But now the gifts, quite appropriately, had dried up. A cold wind was blowing, though the dole kept us fed.

So when a small advert appeared in the *Church Times* seeking the services of a Christian sales executive and naming an improbably generous salary, I leapt. Within a few days I was in London, being thoroughly scrutinised by a West End head-hunter and talking up my rather partial commercial experience at Hodders.[16]

Shortly afterwards I received a call from the London headquarters of World Vision, inviting me for interview.

---

16. I may have over-emphasised my experience as a part-time sales rep.

A date agreed, I asked the cheerful voice on the other end of the line for an exercise, something I could bring to our meeting. 'All right,' said Peter Brierley, clearly entertained. 'We publish the *UK Christian Handbook*. Tell me how you would sell 5,000.'

So began a warm and lasting friendship. Peter Brierley was – and is – a lovely man, a large, jovial gentleman with a booming laugh, and a jobbing mathematician of considerable ability, whose capacity for seeing the story in the numbers has made him a lasting asset to the British Church. Early in our acquaintance he confided to me that as a teenager he would tune out the drearier sermons by calculating the square root of the hymns on the board behind the preacher's head. By background a statistician, he had turned his love of data to a most productive end, assembling – in that pre-Google age – a strikingly useful tool for churches and businesses: the *UK Christian Handbook*.

After quizzing Peter for details, I sat and thought. Then I made a phone call, started our battered red Morris and drove over to the office at All Nations, where I asked the secretary what she thought of it. 'Oh, my goodness,' she said, 'it's a lifeline. You can borrow ours for the weekend, but I want it back.' With this she handed me a chunky purple and yellow volume, much thumbed.

The *Handbook*, published by MARC Europe, a branch of World Vision, brought together in one set of covers information about Christian activities of all kinds: shops, charities, missions, evangelistic agencies, training colleges, church national and regional headquarters, Christian crafts, counselling services, accountants, care homes, insurance firms, car leasing agencies – thousands and thousands of products and services, each with its address, its telephone number, its chief executive and, where available, its turnover.

I turned the pages in astonishment and mounting excitement. Two years' missions training had told me little about the diversity of the UK Church, and this volume painted an unfamiliar picture. So much energy. So many, many people. What a brilliant resource. Starting with his own meticulous address book, Peter had drawn back the curtain on an entire community – a community barely aware of itself. Churches then tended to think in smaller units: I am an Anglican, you are a Baptist. The *Handbook*, which covered all the Trinitarian churches in Britain, celebrated the whole. It was a most valuable piece of practical ecumenism.

Jane and I set to work. I wrote copy, she designed a brochure. The *Handbook* was its own sales tool, listing in its pages the most obvious customers. I had barely heard at that stage of business-to-business marketing, but here it was on a plate. In a pre-digital age every office needed the thing. Any supplier – vendors of photocopiers, for example – would find in such a volume customers with needs they could meet: trustworthy customers, moreover, with a formal adherence to high ethical values and – in theory at least – to paying their bills. The range was exhilarating: any church with a muddle in its accounts or in need of a sound system on a tight budget could find here someone who would not only know what to do, but would *understand*.

The detail was boggling. The *Handbook* was a shocking labour of love, as experience subsequently proved. For every single entry, a form had to be sent out, chased, received, opened, logged, evaluated, queried, abstracted, cross-checked, then filed in such a way that it could be instantly retrieved. (Peter, a man whose soul delighted in complexity, had a labyrinthine filing system of singular precision, which staff were expected to grasp at the outset.[17] We would all need regular refresher courses.) The potential for error was considerable.

The *Handbook* not only linked Christians across the UK, it would also be the germ of another brainwave: the hugely successful Christian Resources Exhibitions, launched by entrepreneur Gospatric Home in 1985, and still going strong. Gospatric always credited Peter's *magnum opus* for sowing the seed.

By the Sunday night I was ready. Jane's beautiful brochure opened my presentation. There was a duplicate copy for Peter, nicely bound. I took the train down to London EC4 the following morning, to the Bible Society's imposing offices, almost immediately opposite The Salvation Army's International HQ in Queen Victoria Street. MARC Europe lived on the fifth floor, sharing space with World Vision of Europe.

A short interview later, Peter offered me the job. I could start in a week.

On my first day at work, I presented myself at Peter's door, suited, booted, and shaved. With a welcoming grin he showed me to my desk, and handed me Jane's brochure. 'Ok,' he told me. 'Do it.'

---

17. The objective of a filing system, as Peter would repeat at the slightest provocation, is not to file things. It's to be able to retrieve them afterwards.

World Vision was then, and remains, one of the world's largest aid agencies, and was among the first to raise funds through the concept of child sponsorship. Started in 1950 by Dr Bob Pierce, an American war correspondent and evangelist, the original purpose of World Vision was to help children orphaned by the Korean War. Its identity was unabashedly Christian, but despite this it has worked successfully with government agencies worldwide. From its American base the work gradually expanded, and in 1982 World Vision UK was established. Now, in the autumn of 1983, I was throwing in my lot with them.

I had thought myself an editor, but my job was sales.

Apart from the *UK Christian Handbook*, which loomed large in the foreground, I had been engaged to sell the range of materials emanating from MARC, a division of World Vision International in Monrovia, CA.

MARC (Missions Advanced Research and Communications) was an unusual outfit. Founded in 1967 by Ed Dayton, it became the organisational structure behind the Lausanne Movement for World Evangelization. Ed Dayton and Peter Brierley were very unalike in person, but they shared a love of good data and sound strategy. Ed's particular enthusiasm was for 'unreached peoples': those who had, as yet, no meaningful chance of hearing the message of salvation.

Such peoples are not simply remote tribes. Every people group (another term much in use at MARC, referring to any group united by ethnicity, profession or status, for example) includes those who have not heard the Good News; by extension, those who are of the same people group will find fewer barriers in reaching them. A London cabbie, runs the theory, will gain a readier hearing among his fellow drivers than will a traffic warden.

A tiny percentage of the considerable income raised for humanitarian work by World Vision was channelled via MARC into the support of missions and the development of thought-through mission strategy, particularly training. To the Christian mind this is legitimate: the care of the body and the care of the soul are one. To be clear, World Vision has a strict rule against proselytising, i.e. requiring anyone to listen to a Christian message before receiving aid: nevertheless, to preach and teach is part of the mission of mercy.

Which is where MARC came in, and to my mind, fresh from All Nations, it seemed a heaven-sent opportunity.

The problem came with the output of the North American office of MARC, which was what I had been employed to sell. Peter showed me volume after volume of carefully described 'unreached people groups', classified by regions of the world. There were drawers of film strips in black canisters, each with a script. It was important, rigorous stuff, mostly generated by a team of serious researchers in California.

The UK market for much of it was perhaps twenty copies.

There was one British component to this unpromising list. Peter had contributed his own densely packed analysis of patterns of churchgoing and belief in Britain, derived from the 1979 English Church Census: a staple-stitched little volume titled *Prospects for the Eighties*. This was more pertinent to my compatriots, but still a pretty recondite little volume, crammed with numbers, with a monochrome cover.

You work with what you have. I called on the Christian Literature Crusade's splendid bookshop in St Paul's Square, round the corner. Mr Page bought a couple of items out of kindness. We were both aware the books would remain on the top shelf until the Second Coming, unless there was a stock clearance.

I went back to my office and stared gloomily at the budget Peter had given me. I was expected to generate £30,000 profit in my first year, and I wasn't sure I could raise a tenth of that. This could be a short-lived adventure. The readers for this esoteric range of books were lecturers and research students at evangelical theological colleges (such as All Nations). The *UK Christian Handbook* usefully listed them all.

I could compile a catalogue and do a mailing, then go back to looking at job adverts.

I sat down to draft some crisp, stimulating copy about the books (who, truly, would want a 400-page, hardback, double-column, statistical assessment of belief patterns among the Inuit?) and laid out a preliminary catalogue. Then I started to think, hard.

During the years at ANCC, we had been given extensive book recommendations on aspects of mission, and this had come to grate on me. Not because the books were not worth buying, but because they were virtually without exception American imports. Mission, as a topic, was hardly tackled by the UK's Christian publishers (it was pretty much ignored by most US publishers too). Mission work was the poor cousin, as far as the UK's churches were concerned: the aftermath of Empire still cast a shadow, and mission = imperialism for many.

However, two years' immersion in the world of missions had shown me a different picture. I had listened enthralled, month after month, to lecturers of vision and ability. Surely the UK had something to say about the task of world mission?

The day after my reality check at CLC I knocked on Peter's door. I laid my concerns before him, and he looked solemn, the expression sitting oddly on his usually cheerful countenance. Then I took a mental deep breath. 'If you will give me the cash,' I told him, 'I will produce a list of books we *can* sell.' I set out some possible titles, some potential authors, focusing on mission and related topics.

A world champion at instant enthusiasm, Peter loved the idea. Within days he had allocated the budget (I did not appreciate until later how generous our distant American directors had been) and the publishing wing of MARC Europe was born.

In the few months following my pivotal meeting with Peter, sleep proved a rare commodity. I was ricocheting between London and Ware, rising early and returning late. In the course of my life I have had the enormous privilege of starting a number of imprints, and establishing a publishing venture from scratch is not straightforward.

For a start, it is capital-intensive. In a healthy publishing programme at least half your annual revenue, probably more, will come from previously published books: the all-important backlist. Conventional wisdom is that it takes nine months to publish a book – assuming that the book arrives ready to edit. We had no backlist, so to get the imprint running required quite significant funds, and Peter had to walk nimbly around the World Vision accountants to obtain the necessary liquidity.

Then there is the problem of list identity. No matter how carefully you frame your mission statement, how extensive your experience, publishing is a creative business, and you find yourself constantly redrafting your guidelines. Your focus is world mission. So books on theory and practice, tick. Other religions, tick. Missionary biographies, tick. What about church planting, or local evangelism? Christian spirituality? Leadership in the local church? Resources for local churches . . . could that include a volume of plays for the church year? All these were actual choices I faced in the first few months.

In addition, if I can put this gently, a new publishing imprint is a magnet for every undiscovered author and every half-completed bestseller.

We had some early successes, nonetheless. Our first volume, a collection of papers presented to a church-planting conference organised by the British Church Growth Association and edited by their secretary Monica Hill, was called, slightly ambitiously, *How to Plant Churches*. Bernard Palmer, editor of the *Church Times* and a valued acquaintance, called in a favour for me and we were delighted when David Edwards, the very distinguished scholar and canon of Westminster Abbey, provided a kind review. We quickly sold our first run and had to reprint.

Martin Goldsmith, lecturer at All Nations and one of the most erudite, charming, and puckish figures in the world of missions, agreed to compile a volume entitled *Love Your Local Missionary*. A short, engaging book, with cartoons by the lovely humourist and priest Taffy Davies, it offered practical advice to churches and was widely taken up by mission agencies.

Dr Eddie Gibbs, a bluff and brilliant academic, then on the staff of the Bible Society and in later years Professor of Church Growth at Fuller Seminary in Pasadena, California, edited *Ten Growing Churches*, which featured ten congregations of note in Britain. This was the first in what proved an enduring series, and also the most successful. *Ten Sending Churches*, edited by Dr Michael Griffiths, the formidable general director of OMF, the Overseas Missionary Fellowship, did very nearly as well. The books were a nightmare to work on, with contributors who knew their stuff but who needed coaxing and guidance to bring out the colour and drama in a potentially stirring account.

Richard Foster, author of the wonderful *Celebration of Discipline*, had written a delightful little volume for IVP US, just a few pages long, entitled *Meditative Prayer*. IVP kindly released the UK rights to us, and with the help of a small advert on the front of the *Church of England Newspaper*, it sold over 40,000 copies in a few months. I had to do some fast footwork to justify its inclusion on the list, theologically speaking, but it was *Richard Foster* . . . of such compromises is the world of publishing made.

One afternoon my phone rang. Stanley Davies, General Secretary of what was then the Evangelical Missionary Alliance (now Global Connections) had an idea to propose. How would I react to a collection of essays from a Christian perspective on the nature and practice of Islam? It would scrupulously adhere to the important principle that you consider other faiths and worldviews in the best possible light. He had just the person to pull it together: Anne Cooper, a former missionary. And so came into being *Ishmael My Brother*, a volume that would stay in print through three editions for over thirty years and prove its worth on training courses worldwide – one year the Urbana conference, a major missions conference in the States, purchased 10,000. It contradicted, incidentally, the common view in the publishing world that collections of articles don't sell.

This was not major league publishing, not at all, but for a young publishing imprint it was an encouraging start.

For the first few books I did everything: commissioning and editing, issuing contracts, discussing terms with printers, meeting designers, finding copy editors and proofreaders, circulating catalogues to bookshops, making sales calls, negotiating discounts, packing orders, typing invoices, and carrying sack after sack of parcels down to the post office. Then Peter took pity on his harried colleague and found me the funds to hire a marketing manager (Malcolm MacLean, an absurdly gifted and quirky salesman and marketeer, who later had a stunning career in magazine publishing). In the course of the next year the team expanded further. Freda Kimmey, a wonderfully effervescent American (later, and for a while, a Franciscan nun), joined the team to oversee book production. Karen Bordeaux, later Karen Barnes – who would one day edit *Good Housekeeping*, among other achievements – handled admin, and Lizzie Gibson – already a prize-winning novelist – joined us as editor. They were capable and eager, and it was a privilege to work with them. On Friday lunchtimes we would repair to the pub to laugh and spin ideas. To my surprise I discovered I was, until Karen joined us, the youngest member of the team.

Under Peter's leadership there was a sense that something important was building. The publishing wing was only one aspect of MARC Europe. We initiated and ran courses on different aspects of leadership, on time management, on church planting, on reaching teenagers. Dioceses and individual churches commissioned Peter to undertake research into needs and contexts. Some of the courses turned into books – Dr David Cormack, a visionary Christian management expert, joined the team, and his skills generated several good volumes including *Seconds Away!*, a book on efficient treatment of people and tasks.[18] David was a bright and shining light who died far too early from cancer: a short, dynamic, and intensely Scottish gentleman whom I was pleased to call a friend.

It quickly became evident that the list was growing to the point where it needed proper commercial representation to the book trade. In what would prove a significant step, I recruited Kingsway to handle our sales, warehousing, and distribution. No more would we have to lug heavy sacks of books to the post.

It is some measure of the intensity of that period that so many details remain so sharp.

Looking back, I made one catastrophic blunder: I was committing us to overheads long before there was a list

---

18. Subtitled *Fifteen rounds in the fight for the effective management of time*, it remains one of the best short books on this essential leadership skill I have read. MARC Europe, Bromley, 1986.

capable of sustaining them. Our vision was greater than our cash flow. It's a common error in publishing start-ups.

Another error was catching up with me.

One morning I received a call from a senior director at Hodders. An author whose work I had acquired, several years previously, was suing the company for breach of contract. Would I be a witness for the defence?

The individual in question, an experienced British sailor and wealthy businessman, had refurbished a large trawler for a life afloat, and had set off on the first leg of a world tour with his wife and three young children. A year later they gave a lift to an ostensibly stranded sailor, who with an accomplice sabotaged the ship's engine. They put into a port in St Lucia for repairs, but their passenger stripped the ship of its many valuables and store of cash while the family was ashore. As the captain and his family subsequently discovered, the thief was essentially a plausible pirate, wanted by police forces around the world, who would be later jailed in the US for stealing a yacht. The book went on to detail a widespread epidemic of piracy around the world.

It was a great story, vividly and engagingly written, with a spiritual aspect: the author and his family professed themselves devout Christians. I loved the book, enjoyed my negotiations with the author, and recommended that we offer a contract. Eric Major accepted the proposal, and when I left Hodders the book was going ahead.

Now, three years later, I discovered the contract had been cancelled and Hodders was being sued. I am still unsure of the grounds for cancellation. Might the story have proved too hot to handle? Out of a sense of loyalty to my old firm, I rather reluctantly agreed to appear in court on their behalf – reluctantly, because my sympathies were torn. In the event I suspect my testimony was barely relevant: Hodders lost the case, and was heavily fined.

I subsequently learned that, in the wake of this event, a warning had been issued to Hodders' editors not to get too close to their authors. Not the legacy I would have wished to leave.

This is a perpetual challenge for editors. In any publishing house the editor is the author's advocate, ensuring the team does a thorough job, representing the author's preferences, acting as a point of liaison. This all works a lot better if relations are cordial. As Edward had amply demonstrated, many authors feel a loyalty to their editor rather than the company.

Yet you have to maintain professional detachment. There will come a day when you need to offer unwelcome counsel; to explain why a marketing initiative will not work; to advise very firmly against a deeply held conviction; to turn down a cherished cover concept; sometimes, even, to insist an advance be repaid. Authors represent the wealth of any publisher, but the publisher is also making an investment. It's the diplomat's dilemma.

Another aspect of this story deserves mention. Hodder & Stoughton was a big company, which made it a big target. Litigation against publishers – for libel, for breach of contract, for breach of copyright – is a fact of life, and the larger the publisher, the more frequent the lawsuits. Any editor needs to be conversant with libel, contract, and copyright law, while making it clear to their authors that they are not qualified to advise.

There are unscrupulous publishers aplenty; there are also unscrupulous authors, and no editor can afford to let down their guard.

Would I today have recommended that Hodders publish that book? Probably not: I was slightly in awe of the storyteller, always a bad sign, and these days I would question whether the book had a sufficiently robust spiritual dimension for inclusion on a Christian list. To the best of my knowledge it has never been published.

The time had come for a move. The Bible Society was selling up, taking advantage of inflated London property prices, and departing from London for Swindon. Peter Brierley took the opportunity to relocate the MARC Europe office: to Bromley, in fact, some nine miles to the south.

For Jane and me, Ware (to the north of London) had only ever been a staging post. We had planned to rent the house there to All Nations College for the use of future students, as and when we set sail for Brazil. Now there was no reason to stay.

We decided to settle in Tunbridge Wells because it was where the South American Missionary Society had its being. Although we were no longer missionaries, we held SAMS in high esteem, and shortly after we arrived Jane was offered a job as their media manager, compiling and editing their newsletter and overseeing their publications programme.

We found ourselves a wonderful Edwardian town house close to the centre of Tunbridge Wells, with six capacious bedrooms distributed over four floors. The elegant staircases would keep us fit, and the extra space could be offered, we thought, to SAMS staff returning on furlough.

We moved happily, with high hopes of a fresh start, but quickly the wheels started to come off our personal wagon.

Our first worry was Abbie. Apart from her slow development, as she grew it became increasingly apparent she was lop-sided: she was developing a scoliosis, a curvature of the spine. This needed urgent attention, or she could end up in a wheelchair and dependent on bottled oxygen. There was no obvious cause for this condition – consultants unhelpfully labelled it as idiopathic, or self-starting – and it was not, so far as anyone could tell, related to her other developmental problems. She had simply been dealt a rotten hand, poor kid.[19]

The common treatment for scoliosis is quite radical surgery; a rod is inserted alongside the spine, which is then wired to it and pulled straight. As the child grows, the surgery has to be repeated. It sounded horrific, and we heard of instances where children had died on the operating table.

There was an alternative: a plaster body cast, to be renewed every four months or so. Under sedation Abbie's crooked frame would be pulled into line, and then immobilised. We chose this option, though it would prove almost as demanding.

This new challenge felt almost too much to bear. Then a friend pointed out that, if we *had* made it to Brazil,

---

19. Idiopathic: a disease or condition the cause of which is not known, or which arises spontaneously.

we should have had to come back within two years for Abbie's medical care, abandoning the work we had gone out to do. It was, perhaps, a severe mercy that our original plans had been derailed. This was a dour and partial comfort, but it made us feel a bit better.

Today I would not embrace such an incoherent view. God is Lord of all, he is author of weal and woe:

I form the light and create darkness,
I bring prosperity and create disaster;
I, the LORD, do all these things.

(Isaiah 45:7, NIV)

Starting when Abbie was five, and for the next eight years or so, Jane or I (but usually Jane) would flog round the M25 on a regular basis to the specialist unit at the Royal National Orthopaedic Hospital in Stanmore, where Abbie's plaster would be replaced. We all found the first cast traumatic: our cheerful squirming youngster had been replaced by a small, vulnerable, top-heavy turtle. She cried and cried, and because her toilet training regressed under the strain, within days the cast stank: she could not bathe. The medical staff were consistently kind and flexible, but the long drive and Abbie's ongoing distress ground us all down. The cast meant she could not run around; she became very tired; and she couldn't understand why we were doing this to her.

Yet the treatment worked, more or less. Abbie is now in her forties, and her back still causes her pain, but she can, with support, live independently. Though there remains an evident kink in her spine, she stands upright; she walks easily; she has survived. Did we make the right choice about treatment? I am not sure.

The other wheel that started to come off was Jane's health.

I had flung myself back into my job, and re-established my identity and sense of purpose. Jane had none of these supports, and was effectively dumped in a strange town without family or friends. The church we chose, though dynamic, did not prove a comfortable fit, run by a minister who relished his self-description as a 'strong natural leader'. Jane's intermittent depression crept in upon her; she contracted alopecia, and to top it all some undeveloped teeth in her upper jaw started to push through, causing considerable pain and ultimately requiring quite extensive dental surgery. In addition, the migraines that had plagued her mother's life now kicked in, and before long every Friday was migraine night, beyond the reach of safe medication.

Of these problems, the hardest for Jane to bear in the long run was her underlying depression. I made matters worse by taking it far too lightly, at least initially. Experience has since taught me that depression is a serious illness, and not amenable to treatment. There is an undercurrent in some Christian cultures that Christians should not get depressed: where is your joy in the Lord, sister? It is amazing how good Christians can be at wounding the wounded.

Despite these burdens, Jane coped well with her job at SAMS, even though there were days when she could barely bring herself to drive to the office. She transformed their newsletter, and cajoled many of their serving staff into sending stories and photos: all part of keeping the mission before the minds, wallets, and praying hearts of supporting churches.

Yet suffering should not be wasted, though I write this with care: when it comes to suffering, I am simply an onlooker.

Mary Craig, the brilliant journalist who wrote *Man from a Far Country*, had four children, two of whom were born with serious genetic defects. Mary, a sensitive woman and a committed Catholic, found the experience simply awful, scarifying to the soul, and she railed at God. Yet she came through it, and would later write that the tragedy of suffering is not the pain, but the wasted opportunity. She called her book about her family *Blessings*. Delia Smith called it 'one of the most moving pieces of writing I have ever read'. It's still available.[20] I met Mary a couple of times, and retain the impression of a vulnerable lady with a tungsten core.

One day Edward England – wearing his literary agent hat – wrote to me with a proposition. His wife Ann had shown him some articles on the care of serving missionaries by Dr Marjory F. Foyle, a doctor and psychiatrist, in an American missions journal. Did I think they would make a book?

With Jane's struggles vividly in mind, I read the material carefully. Dr Foyle had worked in India, Nepal, Pakistan, and Bangladesh. In her series she addressed the whole question of stress among Christian workers, tackling topics such as depression, occupational stress, interpersonal relationships, and burnout. Marjory herself had struggled

---

20. London: Hodder & Stoughton, 1980. Reissued by Canterbury Press, 2012.

with poor mental health, and knew the cost of Christian ministry. At that point, and for years afterwards, she was in demand across the world as a consultant and speaker.

Edward and I agreed terms, and I suggested the title *Honourably Wounded*. The book's calibre was high, but I was worried it might prove too specialised. Two weeks after it was published, Ray Bodkin, Kingsway's financial director, called me urgently. 'We've sold out,' he told me. The first printing of 3,000 copies had vanished in days.

It's a brilliant book, which has sold tens of thousands and stayed in print for nearly thirty years. Missionaries and Christian workers in general put up with a lot, serving for years on low wages, often without thanks. Part of the value of *Honourably Wounded* is that it gives permission for dedicated people to acknowledge they are unwell, and their poor health may be a consequence of their service. As the back cover wording stated, and I still believe, if you put your head above the spiritual parapet, you will get shot at.

Marjory was a gentle, firm, supremely intelligent lady whom I greatly admired. Each year, into her late eighties, she participated in the London marathon in her own way, taking several days to walk the route and relishing every step.

To my surprise, I became the next casualty in our little band.

My health had been good, and I had grown accustomed to thinking of myself as indestructible: the bloke with the energy. This misplaced confidence had taken a blow during the All Nations years, when I had contracted first proctitis and then meningitis, but I was foolishly impatient with such challenges.[21]

One morning, however, I couldn't get out of bed. Flu, I thought, but it got worse. The doctor diagnosed pneumonia, and made daily house calls. 'Don't go to hospital, it's full of sick people, you'll catch something worse,' she told us. Her advice was sound, but I was almost too weak to wash myself. Despite her own fragile health, Jane found herself conscripted as Nurse, trotting up the many stairs to deliver meals I found it almost impossible to keep down, all while coping with two small, lively daughters, one with learning difficulties and trapped in a body cast.

Over the next six weeks I lost almost two stones. For several weeks I was really unwell. As I started to recover, Jane and I took stock. The house was too big, the garden too small, the location too urban. There was no local community to speak of. One day, as Jane drove us through the Kentish lanes in a bid to escape the hospital atmosphere, we spotted a thatched cottage for sale in the nearby village of Stockland Green. Old Thatch would become our new home for a couple of years before we moved to the larger nearby village of Speldhurst. Speldhurst had (and still has) an excellent junior school, which would soon be relevant for Carrie. We would stay there for over a decade, making friends to treasure, and getting deeply involved in the parish church.

---

21. A story told in *Taking My God for a Walk*, p 42f

I wanted to put my All Nations training to work. I enquired about becoming a Reader in the Church of England, and – in the more informal manner of that period – was quizzed by the Diocesan Warden of Readers about the course we had undertaken, then told: write three essays, and we'll license you.[22] Today the training is far more rigorous.

The rector of Speldhurst, Geoffrey Hyder, put a brave face on the matter and let me loose on his three congregations in the united parish. Geoffrey, in fact, gave me the only useful training I received, listening to a dry run sermon from the back of the church and taking me through the rhythms of Morning Prayer and Evensong. 'Keep the sermon down to twelve and a half minutes,' he insisted. Unless you are very, very good, that is quite long enough.

At the retreat before my licensing, the speaker, Dr Chris Wright, told us to keep a piece of towelling in the pocket of our cassocks.[23] 'Your job is to wash the disciples' feet,' he said. 'Never forget it.' Jane slipped a morsel of cloth into my pocket when we got home that night. It stayed with me for decades.

We published some dozens of books over the next few years under the MARC Europe label.

Despite the output, I started to find the guidelines for the imprint chafing. This came into sharp focus when I

---

22. Readers in the C of E are licensed to teach and preach, and, with additional training, to officiate at funerals.
23. For some years the Principal of All Nations, and now a distinguished author.

made my first trip to the States, to visit MARC's American head office. Missionaries and charity executives all, they had never previously included a commercial publisher on the team, and I fitted in with all the elegance of a warthog singing arias. Nevertheless they made me welcome, and one evening my American counterpart, a kindly academic, took me to hear the distinguished psychiatrist M. Scott Peck, author of the astonishingly wise *The Road Less Travelled*[24] and *People of the Lie*.

A year or so after publishing *The Road Less Travelled*, Peck had resolved his own spiritual pilgrimage by being baptised into the Protestant faith, and *The People of the Lie* reflected this journey. On hearing this (and very impressed by both the man and his books) I contacted the American publishers and acquired UK and Commonwealth rights to both titles.

At which point Peter Brierley stepped in and categorically refused to sign the contracts. Peck's books were just too far outside our boundaries; they could simply not be held in the same brackets as our commission to produce materials assisting in the task of world mission. Argue as I might, I could not carry the day. With a very poor grace I wrote and turned the books down.

Decades later the decision still rankles. Peter was absolutely right to keep me focused: I was not engaged to build a publishing empire. Yet *The Road Less Travelled* went on to sell over ten million copies, an enormous bestseller on both sides of the Atlantic and right around the world. Had we acquired the rights it would probably have transformed our finances.

---

24. First released in 1978. Published in the UK by Ebury.

The incident brought all too vividly to mind an earlier conversation with Edward England. As a man with my faltering steps set on the road to simplicity, I had read and esteemed *Small is Beautiful* by E.F. Schumacher, subtitled *A study of economics as if people mattered*, and considered by the *Times Literary Supplement* in 1995 to be 'one of the 100 most important books published since World War II'.[25] Schumacher, a distinguished economist, and an adult convert to Catholic faith, slammed the idea that growth is always good, ridiculed the notion of gross national product as a measure of happiness, and promoted the radical concept of 'enoughness': appropriate technology, sustainable development. A prophet greatly honoured, Schumacher's death from a heart attack in 1977, at the age of sixty-six, deprived the world of a visionary.

Edward and his senior colleagues shook their heads at Schumacher's teaching: altogether too subversive. So when, on Schumacher's unexpected demise, I eagerly proposed that we quickly commission a biography, the idea fell absolutely flat, leaving me biting my desk in frustration. Schumacher's daughter Barbara Wood published her father's biography a few years later, and it proved highly popular: it is still available.

Let me not mislead. These books would have succeeded, but so many have failed. Over the years I have published many fine volumes, and one or two really major bestsellers. I have also published hundreds which failed to make the grade. Few are so dangerous as the man who thinks he knows what he is doing.

---

25. First released in 1973. Published in the UK by Vintage.

Peter could not have been unaware of my frustration over *The Road Less Travelled*, because he left the reins pretty slack thereafter. One consequence of this was *Laughter in Heaven*.

I cannot now recall what dubious rationale I offered my boss for this collection of sketches from playwright Murray Watts, one of the founders of The Riding Lights Theatre Company, co-author of *Time to Act*, and by now a personal friend. It was scarcely germane to the task of world mission, but it was undoubtedly fun. However, it presented a problem. How could we, with our slender resources, give this new volume anything like the profile of its predecessor?

I passed the challenge to Malcolm MacLean, who thought about it for a day, then came back to me with a masterstroke.

The Greenbelt Festival was rolling round again.[26] How would it be, suggested Malcolm, if we rented a small zeppelin, an airship, which could be tethered outside the massive book tent to advertise our title? The cost was not extortionate, but it would consume the whole of the book's meagre marketing budget. With mingled enthusiasm and trepidation – Malcolm's ideas could be outrageous – I agreed to the plan.

It paid off wonderfully. The airship duly arrived, adorned with the banner Malcolm had commissioned, proclaiming *Laughter in Heaven*. It soared visible right across the site, swaying in the breeze high above our heads and marking

---

26. The annual Greenbelt Festival is a Christian-based festival of the arts, held under canvas each August.

to all the location of the book tent. Bowing to my urgent entreaty, the bookstall manager had ordered substantial stocks. That weekend we sold at least nine hundred copies, and Murray was delighted.

In book marketing there is a great deal of hard graft and attention to detail: writing copy, designing covers, soliciting endorsements, contacting reviewers, suggesting speakers, and ensuring metadata details are accurate. Blogs, Facebook pages, Twitter feeds, TikTok clips and the rest all have their place, as does the careful maintenance of links with journalists and producers. Such things are the bread and butter of good marketing. But what is beyond value is the imaginative leap, the lightbulb idea, the quirk, the inspired title or event or pairing that lifts the book from the ruck, and attaches wings to its feet.

Inspired titles come in all forms. One of the most popular books we published during the MARC Europe years was *Don't Let the Goats Eat the Loquat Trees*. An account by an American surgeon, Tom Hale, of his dramatic, occasionally gruesome and frequently hilarious adventures in Nepal, the book had been sent to me by a contact at the American publishers Zondervan. If you imagine James Herriot translated to the world of Nepalese medicine, you won't be far off the mark. I read it with delight, and the book did well – but it contained very little about goats, and almost nothing about loquat trees. There has been a fashion in recent years for more prosaic, does-what-it-says-on-the-tin titles, in an effort to register with search engines, but the results are so often *dull*.

The publishing programme was forging ahead, but all was not well at MARC Europe. Despite our best efforts –

publishing, researching, running conferences, providing consultancy services – we were still, several years on, dependent on subsidies from World Vision, and funds were drying up.

In 1984 the news of the Ethiopian famine – the consequence of failing rainfall, disastrous agricultural policies, and civil war – had shaken the world. In late October, the BBC television news reports of Michael Buerk and cameraman Mohamed Amin had galvanised a huge international response. In November of that year Bob Geldof and other stars recorded 'Do They Know It's Christmas?' The following July Geldof organised the ground-breaking Live Aid concerts, watched by more than 400 million people worldwide. Money poured in from around the globe, and World Vision, competent and efficient, was well placed to administer funds and deliver aid to the starving millions in the Horn of Africa.

Now, in 1987, the flood of cash had slowed dramatically. The expression 'donor fatigue' emerged. The need remained urgent, but people around the world (and particularly in America) were weary of giving, and charities large and small had to retrench, abandoning projects, cutting back. Our parent body acted decisively, reducing staff worldwide and slashing overheads. It was a painful time: around the world over a thousand people lost their jobs at World Vision.

As our funding disappeared, MARC Europe headed for the financial abyss, and our trustees had to do what was necessary. The publishing operation, which had the highest overheads and the most unreliable income, found itself in the firing line. With tears in his eyes Peter shared the bad news. The team I had built up over the previous four years was given its cards. We hugged one another in grief: we had worked so hard, but the numbers could not be gainsaid. It is really not easy to start a publishing house from scratch.

It was a tiny tragedy, not to be compared with what was happening in Africa. Other staff members were also axed. Peter hung on doggedly, working long hours to retrieve what he could, and in following years his passion for good statistics gave rise to a new body, Christian Research.

I, too, was made redundant. As one of my last acts before leaving I engineered the sale of MARC Europe's publishing wing to Kingsway, which was already handling our distribution. Kingsway bought everything: the MARC Europe imprint, the stock, dozens of future contracts. The deal released badly needed funds for Peter's struggling operation. There was one important exception, however: the *UK Christian Handbook* and its companion volumes, over which Peter retained control.[27]

In autumn 1987 Kingsway offered me a position on their board. Geoff Ridsdale, their managing director, had plans for expansion.

---

27. Under the MARC Europe imprint Peter had published several different handbooks: *The Netherlands Christian Handbook, The French Christian Handbook, The Finnish Christian Handbook,* etc. The UK edition would become an important part of the ongoing work of Christian Research.

8

Kingsway

It was good to be part of a fully focused publishing operation again. I had valued my time at MARC Europe, and had learned a lot, but Kingsway was the real deal.

These days Kingsway is no more, subsumed into David C Cook. However, in the late 1980s Kingsway Books and Music formed an influential part of the British Christian scene. It published the hugely popular *Songs of Fellowship*, hymnal of choice for millions; it handled the work of many outstanding Christian musicians, including Graham Kendrick (whose album *Shine Jesus Shine* was released shortly after I arrived); and its books division, headed by Richard Herkes, put forth a stream of successful authors. It was a rare week we did not have several titles in the national Christian bestseller lists.

Richard – a quietly spoken, shrewd man, with an academic background in philosophy – was more than gracious. He cannot have been well pleased to learn that a bouncy ex-Hodders editor was to join him on the board, but he showed me the ropes and bore patiently with my intrusive questions.

In September 1988 we started a new company. The MARC imprint was too small a fish: too specialised and limited to hold its own alongside its larger cousin.

We decided to create Monarch Publications Ltd as a subsidiary of The Servant Group, which owned Kingsway. Monarch, we hoped, might challenge the market leader Lion, publishing Christian books for a wider readership. Under Monarch's wing would fall MARC, still focusing on mission and church growth, and there would be a further new imprint, Minstrel, to handle fiction, drama and humour: the world of Christian arts.

Richard Herkes retained oversight of Kingsway; I focused on Monarch. However, we quickly found ourselves working on books more suitable for the other's patch. It rarely works well to switch a book from one editor to another, as the relationship between author and editor is critical to the success of the enterprise. So Richard edited some titles on the Monarch programme; I did the same for Kingsway.

Monarch got off to a respectable start, but it was quickly clear that its subsidiary Minstrel had far greater potential. In the course of the next three years we would release, under Minstrel, Adrian Plass's *Clearing Away the Rubbish*; Murray Watts' first volume of Christian jokes, *Rolling in the Aisles*; and the two Frank Peretti blockbusters, *This Present Darkness* and *Piercing the Darkness*. In 1990, Monarch turned over more than £600,000: it would take years for the imprint to reach this point again.

Adrian Plass, a huge, lovely, gentle but troubled man, had drawn upon his own wry spirit for *The Sacred Diary of Adrian Plass Aged 37 3/4*, which had been released by Marshall Pickering in 1987. It would sell well over a million copies, and Adrian's star was riding high. Richard and Adrian had been friends for years, and Richard scored a major coup in persuading Adrian to place his new book with us. *Clearing Away the Rubbish*, a collection of shorter pieces, full of wit and tenderness, was one of Minstrel's first releases, and contained some of Adrian's most delightful monologues. Demand was predictably high.

Murray's *Rolling in the Aisles* was less predictable. Christian humour remains one of the trickiest areas, with many a reader quick to take offence. The slightest innuendo, the lightest touch of irreverence, and letters came pouring in. Perhaps the greatest gap lies in mid-Atlantic, with American customers, then and now, swift to rise in outrage at their degenerate old country cousins.

Response to Murray's book was forthright. It sold in lorryloads, in tens of thousands, but the letters of complaint streamed in. I treasure the memory of one particular week, when two letters arrived from church elderships which had met specifically to discuss just how far *Rolling in the Aisles* had overstepped the boundaries. Each made much the same point: 'We consider ourselves to have a strong sense of humour[28] and the following jokes we would regard as genuinely funny . . . However, the following give grave cause for concern, and we are dismayed that a responsible publishing company such as yourselves . . . (etc.).' Both letters contained lists of jokes, acceptable and unacceptable.

There was no overlap between the lists.

---

28. Avoid anyone who says this.

Outrage is a familiar flavour to Christian publishers, at least to anyone foolhardy enough to publish anything close to the bone. Christian booksellers have a hard time of it, of course, being a ready target for the disgruntled of this parish. When we released *101 Things to Do During a Dull Sermon* by Tim Sims and Dan Pegoda, I had expected mild interest: we sold thousands, and the book stayed in print for decades.[29] This didn't stop a rather ugly showdown at the sales conference following publication when two members of the team, who had been given serious earache by their bookshops, demanded I stop publishing such material in sufficiently forceful terms to give me a facial tic for years afterwards.[30]

Of all the books I have ever published, I think *101 Things to Do During a Dull Sermon* provoked the strongest reaction. Originally published by the (now defunct) *Wittenberg Door,* a satirical Christian magazine from Texas, it gently mocked the pretensions and misunderstandings associated with the preacher's role. The challenge is that for many Christians the proclamation of the word is a sacred matter.[31] But the bombast, ineptitudes, and absurdities of preachers do need exposure, and here the problem lies. I think this book has generated more personal abuse than any other I have handled. *Caveat venditor.*

I can take no credit for acquiring the astonishingly successful Peretti novels: they were bought from the American publisher Crossway by Richard Herkes.

---

29. I later bought the rights again for Lion Hudson, after Kingsway let the book go out of print, and it went through several further printings.
30. I didn't.
31. Actually I agree. The distinction surely lies between the Message and the messenger: to twit the latter is not to mock the former. Lose this distinction and you are in trouble.

This Present Darkness, first released in 1986, is a Christian horror fantasy. It depicts the battle for the soul of a small American town, between the forces of light and the powers of darkness. Unseen armies of archangels and demon lords are empowered or brought low by the worship, intercessions or failings of the faithful. It's gripping stuff, and to date has sold well over two million copies worldwide. Like its successor, the almost equally successful *Piercing the Darkness*, it dramatises the battle in the heavenlies which, many believe, takes place when a Christian falls to their knees.

Many read them as prayer manuals. We sold hundreds of thousands of each in the first year of publication.

For a brief while we thought we had cracked it. With hard countable evidence that Christian fiction could sell, we started buying rights from American publishers, and commissioning fiction ourselves.

What I had failed to appreciate was that Peretti's novels were not truly being read as fiction; instead they should be perceived as expressions of popular spirituality (a more recent equivalent would be William Paul Young's *The Shack*). Their popularity said little about Christian fiction as a genre: these books are more properly located on the same shelf as *The Pilgrim's Progress*.

This did not mean Christian fiction wasn't viable; just that different rules applied.

At that period, as today, the American market for Christian fiction was far more developed than its equivalents elsewhere. American novels intended for Christian readership have poured forth, with subgenres such as prairie romances and Amish fiction playing an important role. Many of these books really sell only in the States, though in eye-watering numbers.

In the UK, Christian fiction sells reasonably well in Northern Ireland, and to a degree in Scotland; in England it has been tough going, and far less successful in numerical terms than, say, Christian biography or books on Christian living. My own explanation for this is that in Northern Ireland and Scotland there are still Christian communities of sufficient strength that the faith permeates the culture, and fiction written with believers in mind feels quite comfortable, not too far a stretch. By contrast, in those parts of the world (including much of England) where faith is tough and Christians are a mocked minority, some parts of the Church have perceived the idea of Christian novels, I think, as a bit fluffy. The task of holding fast to your Saviour is just too serious.

However, this is an error of perception. Good fiction tells the truth more surely and more fully than nonfiction; a great story will carry truth past the watchful dragons of the mind, in C.S. Lewis's memorable phrase. The door of the imagination is for many people the most helpful entry point to the gospel. That's why Jesus told parables.

Today this regional variation has become less important, with (particularly in respect of fiction) the growth of eBooks, and access (at the time beyond easy reach for British publishers) to the American market. But at that point, in the late 1980s Christian bookshops controlled the marketplace, and obviously could not afford to stock titles that didn't move. By 1995 I would abandon the world of fiction, and would not return to it for a decade.

All that came later. One day in 1989 my friend Richard Martin appeared at my office door. At that point Richard, who would go on to develop a considerable music business, Classic Fox, was employed by Kingsway to handle overseas sales. He lived along the coast in Hastings, where he rented a room.

'My landlady wrote this,' he told me, inconsiderately adding a wodge of paper to my overflowing in-tray. 'I've read it, and it's great. See what you think.'

I eyed the new addition sceptically. Friends of friends are something of an occupational hazard for commissioning editors, but I respected Richard's judgement. Always listen to your sales team. I took the typescript home, and after supper and the children's bedtime I settled down to read, with a whiskey at my elbow.

The Hawk and the Dove, by Penelope Wilcock, is the first in a trilogy of books we published over the next two years. Set in a medieval monastery in Yorkshire, at around the time of Chaucer, they recount the life and death of Abbot Peregrine, a man who demonstrates great intellect and integrity, but who wrestles with arrogance and impatience. Pen Wilcock (who had once considered a calling to monastic life) wanted to show how monks, vowed to poverty, celibacy, and obedience, and moreover from a century far different from our own, could nevertheless struggle with exactly the same anxieties and aggravations: finding our niche; coping with failure; living with impossible people; making amends when we realise we are the impossible ones. The monks discover, in the daily rhythm of their work and worship, that the whole of life is a love story, about a tender and passionate God.

Utterly won over, I persuaded my colleagues to publish it. The three volumes sold modestly in the UK, but Crossway picked the series up for the US market and it remains in print to this day, having sold in tens of thousands. At least one American high school developed a curriculum around the trilogy.[32]

The books side of things was doing well, but Kingsway's music division was really the engine of the company (especially the highly profitable song-publishing concern, Thankyou Music, pioneered by Geoff Shearn and Nigel Coltman). David Nickalls, head of production, himself a capable musician, oversaw the task of setting and proofreading the music for *Songs of Fellowship*, the company's songbook. Like *Sound of Living Waters* before it – and *Mission Praise* from Marshall Pickering – it rode a wave of new worship, fuelled by the enthusiasm of the charismatic movement.

The leader of Kingsway Music was John Paculabo, a blunt Liverpudlian. Originally a singer-songwriter, John and his band Parchment hit the charts in the early seventies with 'Light Up the Fire'. John later joined Kingsway as Director of Music. He and his team had a talent for spotting songs (finds included 'In Christ Alone' and 'Here I Am To Worship') and Christian worship worldwide owes him a considerable debt.

John was a shrewd, ebullient, burly bloke with a refreshingly candid approach to life and a genius for developing great artists. His job required him to listen to

---

32. There are now nine volumes in the series, but start with the trilogy. See Chapter 9 for more detail.

the dozens of tapes which poured into our offices from aspiring musicians. One morning, going past his door, I found myself wincing at the discordant blasts from the tape deck in his room.

'Why don't you buy yourself a halfway decent sound system?' I queried.

John grinned at me through his bushy beard. 'It's awful,' he agreed, ejecting a cassette. 'But look at it this way. If I come across something that still sounds good through my system, then it's *good*.'

A few months later I noticed a crowd around his door, and moving closer was caught up in the sheer exuberance of the beat. When the tape ended, John beamed at us. 'Isn't it great? It's called *Trad Jazz Praise*.'

Of all the excellent albums he masterminded, that remains a favourite. You can find it on Spotify.

John died of cancer in 2013, aged just sixty-six.

One day I received a phone call.

'Nick Jones here,' said a precise, cultured voice. 'Can Angus and I come and see you?'

A week later Angus Hudson and Nick arrived. Angus and his fellow director ran Angus Hudson Ltd, which Nick had helped Angus to acquire in a management buyout from the British Printing Corporation. The pair were astute, visionary, committed. They made a memorable couple: Angus small, florid, animated, and polished; Nick vast, serious and, on that first occasion, almost entirely silent.

The premise behind their business was that colour publication is expensive. Good artwork costs a lot; full colour printing costs a lot. But if you restrict the text to black ink, you can print all the images at once, and then go back and run the entire edition through the presses again, filling in the text in different languages and achieving valuable economies of scale. The process is called co-editing or co-publishing, and it's a well-established practice.

However, it takes a lot of time, care, and patience to organise, and Angus and Nick spotted an opportunity. Both were inveterate networkers, men of diligence and good humour, with considerable natural authority. Angus was the upfront negotiator, while Nick kept a close eye on the numbers. They had a formidable list of international contacts, which they guarded jealously.

Their proposal to me that day was that Kingsway should publish a new edition of the *Student Bible Atlas* by Tim Dowley. Tim, a well-regarded historian of the church, together with Pat Alexander, had organised and edited an immensely successful Lion handbook, *The History of Christianity*.[33]

Scripture Union, Angus explained, had published an edition of the *Atlas* a few years earlier, but it had not done well, and he had bought the rights back. Kingsway had an altogether larger sales operation: would we like to have a go?

I was fascinated. The *Atlas* is a short, deceptively simple document, summarising in thirty colourful maps the context of the Old and New Testaments. The Bible is full

---

33. There was a longstanding friendship between Angus Hudson and Lion: Angus had helped David and Pat Alexander, who founded Lion, to print the ground-breaking *Lion Handbook to the Bible*.

of epic journeys – Abraham's travels from Ur to the land of Canaan; the Hebrews' long road from slavery in Egypt to the Promised Land; Paul's missionary endeavours around the Mediterranean. Any Bible student would find the *Atlas* valuable. I was sure we could make a success of it, and signed the contract.

Despite my blithe confidence, the book was an anomaly on Kingsway's list, and though we profited from Nick's international contacts, the shops evinced little interest. I failed to communicate to our team where the market might be found, and our sales were modest. A few years after I had left, Kingsway reverted rights, and Nick (who took over as CEO of Angus Hudson Ltd when Angus retired) published it himself, using it as the cornerstone for a series of such books. Under his guiding hand the *Atlas* ultimately sold hundreds of thousands of copies, in over thirty languages.

It matters greatly that a book should have the right home.

That was my first meeting with Nick, one of publishing's giants. We would work together many times in the years ahead.

Early in 1990 another phone call opened an entirely new vista.

'Nicky Gumbel here,' announced a smooth, authoritative voice. 'I work with HTB. I've written a little booklet. We've been photocopying it, but I think we need a publisher. Could you be interested?'

Nicky Gumbel, a former barrister with an impeccable background (Eton and Cambridge), was at that point a curate at Holy Trinity Brompton, widely known as HTB. The vicar at HTB, Sandy Millar, had asked Nicky to take over the running of a course for enquirers, called the Alpha Course, and one of Nicky's early initiatives was to write a little booklet of sixteen pages, called *Why Jesus?*

The little booklet duly arrived, illustrated with cartoons by Charlie Mackesy, a friend of the author.[34]

Booklets are not usually welcomed by bookshops. They are cheap, lack a spine, and take up space which could be more profitably used by other titles. However, Kingsway had some experience with booklets. A few years previously it had acquired Falcon Books, an imprint which included *Journey into Life* by another Anglican minister, Norman Warren, which offers a pictorial account of making a decision to follow Jesus, and ends with the 'Sinner's Prayer'. When, as a teenager, I went forward at a Billy Graham meeting, a copy of *Journey into Life* was pressed into my hands. *Journey into Life* – also a volume of sixteen pages – was first published in 1964, and has sold at least thirty million worldwide. It has been translated into dozens of languages. Kingsway sold *Journey into Life* in packs of ten, and demand was high. Many churches would order regular supplies.

At that point the Alpha Course was still in its infancy. Comprising twelve sessions on the basics of Christian belief, it had started in 1977, but had not really caught on. When Nicky took the helm, just four courses were running at HTB, but that was about to change: in 1998 over 10,000

---

34. Charlie Mackesy, a distinguished and successful artist, is author of the celebrated *The Boy, the Mole, the Fox and the Horse*, Waterstone's Book of the Year in 2019.

were held in Britain, and Alpha was advertised on buses across the country. The momentum has continued: by 2018 Alpha was running in over a hundred countries and languages.

We agreed to print a modest few thousand of his little booklet, at 50p each. The first run sold in days, and within a month or two, Nicky and I were working on *Questions of Life*, which would become the staple book behind the Alpha Course. Other bestsellers followed.

I'd like to be able to take credit for acquiring for Kingsway what would prove one of its most valuable assets, but in truth I simply answered the phone.

On 16 August 1990 a fire swept through the STL warehouse in Carlisle, destroying a vast stock of Christian books and CDs, including everything published by Kingsway and Monarch.

The disaster heralded a turning point for the company. Ray Bodkin, the deeply respected and prescient financial guru for The Servant Group, had doubled our fire insurance weeks previously, so we had the wherewithal to get ourselves back on our feet. The fire could have been a source of blessing – a wonderfully direct way of dealing with overstocks – but in fact it precipitated a crisis.

Over the previous four or five years the company had expanded, taking on expensive additional staff (such as me) and increasing its output. We had moved to new premises, though we had failed to find a tenant for the old ones. Turnover was sharply up, but so were overheads, and not everything we touched turned to gold. Cash flow was tight. Geoff Ridsdale, our chief executive, had been shocked by the levels of stress he found at the company when he took over the reins a few years previously, and had tried to expand his way to resilience, but the bold ploy was faltering.

The fire at STL precipitated a very hard look at the company's books, which told a woeful story, and Geoff ultimately resigned. We could no longer stave off the looming financial crisis, and I had my first experience of making good colleagues redundant.

During this period, all was not well at home. Abbie's education had proved a particular challenge, requiring a couple of school moves: special needs education was, as so often, something of a Cinderella, and the provision in Kent wasn't brilliant. Carrie was doing better, making friends, finding her feet at secondary school, and showing real artistic talent.

However, Jane's depression was gaining on her. I was caught up in my world, leaving early and returning late, often monosyllabic and fogged with fatigue. Jane had made good friends in the village, but there were days when I would come home to find her weeping and stir-crazy with loneliness.

Casting around for something she could make her own, I suggested we set up a Christian literary agency. This struck a spark. Jane undertook a brief course offered by the local chamber of commerce on how to run your own company, and 'Collins and Collins' was born. In the event it would prove a short-lived affair, soon overtaken by other developments, but it lodged within us the idea that we should run our own business.

After Geoff resigned, The Servant Group was left rudderless. Ray Bodkin, John Paculabo, and I sat down in Ray's office for a chat. Ray made it plain he didn't want to take the helm, and no one else was stepping forward. John and I went back to his office and talked some more. 'How would it be,' I suggested to him, 'if I back you for the top job, and you sell me Monarch?'

Within months the deed was done. It was an easy negotiation: Kingsway got rid of a senior executive, and turned stock into cash. John and Pem Bridger, Jane's parents, astonishingly[35] mortgaged their house to provide the down payment, and John Pac and I agreed a three-year schedule for the balance. The stock would remain at STL's rebuilt facility in Carlisle; Kingsway's sales team would continue to represent the range. The lucrative Minstrel list, as the non-executive directors hastened to make clear, was not on the table, but the lesser Monarch and MARC imprints were available, and after crunching the numbers, I thought we could make a go of it.[36]

---

35. Astonishingly, because a) it was incredibly generous; b) they knew nothing about publishing; c) Jane was one of four daughters, and her three younger siblings had a claim on any available funds; and d) her parents had no time whatsoever for the Christian faith. But they were lovely Cornish people, intelligent and kind, always ready at journey's end with a single malt and a delectable homemade pasty, and I treasure their memory.
36. Sadly, the Minstrel imprint became something of an orphan at Kingsway, and would wither on the vine.

In December 1991 we signed the papers. John took over Kingsway, and Jane and I became proud owners of our own publishing company. Monarch was ours.

9

Monarch

For the first years of our joint enterprise things went remarkably well. We urgently compiled a catalogue of new books, and presented our first list to the Kingsway sales team just a couple of months later.

Early on we were fortunate enough to acquire British rights to books by two American authors, C. Peter Wagner and Neil T. Anderson. Both were men of enormous ability, both with a solid scholarly background, and both had stepped out from the objectivity of the academic world to develop a significant and controversial public ministry.

C. Peter Wagner, who served for thirty years as Professor of Church Growth at Fuller Theological Seminary in California, had published a string of valuable books about the church growth movement, but now he was branching out into more contentious areas. In our first couple of years we published *Warfare Prayer*, swiftly followed by *Prayer Shield*. Both sold in excess of 10,000, and we were well pleased. Gradually, however, I became uneasy with his more adventurous theories, such as spiritual mapping, territorial spirits, and strategic-level spiritual warfare, and he didn't reply when I wrote to ask him for biblical and contemporary evidence. This summary doesn't do him justice, and interested readers should test his books for themselves, but after two or three years we decided that we simply couldn't publish his further volumes with integrity.

I had been here before. Years previously, at Hodders, I had published British editions of Ruth Carter Stapleton's *The Gift of Inner Healing* and *The Experience of Inner Healing.* Ruth, the sister of US President Jimmy Carter, had a significant ministry as an evangelist, but her convictions concerning healing of the memories (the counselee visualises Jesus coming into the darkest situations, and ministering directly to their wounded inner child) gradually soared off into the whimsical, and I had to recommend to my colleagues that we should not continue to publish her.

What can you do when a successful author goes spiralling off into make-believe? Part of an editor's function is to ask awkward questions, fully aware that to do so may damage the relationship for good.

Neil Anderson, too, has had his critics, particularly among those who disapprove profoundly of the charismatic movement, but Neil's work is more obviously biblically based. In 1992 and 1993 we brought out his two seminal volumes, *Victory Over the Darkness* and *The Bondage Breaker*, and they sold printing after printing.

Neil's basic idea is that Christ has set us entirely free, so that we are released from our past, from other people's agendas, from malign forces. We may be saved, but to acknowledge Christ as Saviour and Lord is only the start of the process – it is as if we have sidled through the Pearly Gates, but stay perched just over the threshold. As we allow Christ's love and power to penetrate to our core, so we are set free to grow in Him, to become who we were meant to be, to live fully and gloriously according to the Maker's instructions.

To spread these ideas he had set up Freedom in Christ Ministries.

Neil was a burly, delightful, and slightly awe-inspiring figure, a former aerospace engineer turned theologian, a dedicated golfer with five earned degrees, two doctorates, and a background as a wrestling coach. At the height of his fame, I met him one year at the Christian Booksellers' Association annual convention in the States. Here was an author whose books sold in seven figures, yet he was content to spend a day wandering the convention floor and chatting to all.

A couple of years after we had published *The Bondage Breaker*, Neil and his wife Joanne came to England on a short speaking tour.[37] I met them in Reading, and Neil wanted my opinion. 'A young couple have asked me if they can develop a British branch of Freedom in Christ. They seem serious. Can you talk to them for me?'

It was thus that I first met Steve and Zoë Goss. A few years later, Steve proposed a course to give Christians of all ages and stages the spiritual grounding Neil's ideas had outlined. Published in 2004 as the Freedom in Christ Course, this proved a big hit: it is now available worldwide, in thirty-five languages at the time of writing. Steve would later succeed Neil as president of Freedom in Christ

---

37. Neil was keen to visit our offices, so that 'My people can meet your people'. At that point Monarch consisted of Jane and me, working from our spare bedroom. I scraped together an excuse.

International, and under his leadership the movement is flourishing. I'll come back to this.

By this point Jane, Abbie, Carrie, and I had moved to Owl Lodge, a larger house in the centre of Speldhurst, and it was here we set up shop. The purchase of Monarch immediately gave me back two hours a day, the grind to Eastbourne relegated to memory. For a few months we had our fax machine plugged into a socket in our bedroom, until we found we could not prevent ourselves jumping out of bed in the small hours to inspect orders arriving from Australia or South Africa.

It was absurdly exciting. I no longer had to convince a dozen colleagues about the merits of an author, or attend contentious meetings about cover designs and print runs. The risks and rewards were entirely ours. We were free. Our task was simple: to sort the wheat from the husk.

Those first two years were reminiscent of the early days of MARC Europe: everything seemed possible. We were making enough money, approximately. Jane's depression receded, and to my delight she became caught up in the adventure of books. We kept our overheads right down, only employing a part-time administrator (Nicky Rees, still a valued friend).

That first summer we published Jane Grayshon's wonderful *Confessions of a Vicar's Wife*, a rococo collection of selected absurdities which sold a quick 20,000. It sat oddly alongside the spiritual warfare and the books on revival and mission, but hey.

Another improbable venture was Ram Gidoomal's *Sari 'n' Chips*. Ram arrived in the UK in his teens. Born into a

Hindu family, brought up in the Sikh faith, and educated at a Muslim school in Kenya, Ram became a Christian believer as a young adult. A brilliant businessman, he made a fortune in the food industry and retired at the age of forty. Since then he has stood to become London's mayor, served as chair of Traidcraft and the Lausanne Movement, and so much else: he has been appointed CBE and Freeman of the City of London. He is a spokesman for Britain's powerful Asian community.

Which makes it all the more unexpected that in 1992 he found his way to our door, with a proposal for an autobiography focusing on the East-meets-West aspect of his remarkable life. With Ram behind it, the book did well: his connections were superb, and a photo of John Major, then Prime Minister, holding *Sari 'n' Chips* aloft, appeared in *The Times of India*. I doubt whether Sir John remembers the incident.

Sometimes you get a chance to put something right. While working at Kingsway, I had received a book from a friend at the American company Fleming H Revell. *His Needs, Her Needs* by Willard Harley, subtitled rather provocatively *Building an affair-proof marriage*, described ten needs shared by men and women: admiration, affection, an attractive spouse, conversation, domestic support, family commitment, financial support, honesty and openness, recreational companionship, and sexual fulfilment. The needs are similar, but the sequence varies: how would you prioritise them?

It looked promising, but it was one of many similar volumes which arrived in those years from the States on the art of marriage, and didn't make it to the top of the pile. Other British publishers also ignored it.

Now it occurred to me I might have blundered. A quick fax to Fleming Revell (now an imprint of Baker Book House) confirmed rights were available. The American edition was still in hard cover, so we released a paperback.

Which, to my astonishment, captured the British imagination. Today, several revisions later, it still figures on bestseller lists, with translations into over twenty languages and world sales in excess of three million. It's a fine book.

The publishing was thrilling, but the deliveries were not. We lived at the end of a narrow lane, and time after time an unexpected item of overseas mail would turn up, a modest parcel carried by some behemoth of an articulated lorry, which would then reverse, carving ruts in lawns and crushing hedges.

To pacify our apoplectic neighbours we sought alternative accommodation. A pub round the corner had an unused room, for a peppercorn rent, and to our entire satisfaction we conducted our business for the next couple of years from this small mouse-ridden unit, walking down each day to the village post office to send out the mail. I loved the idea of cutting-edge world-changing Christian literature emerging from a little Kentish pub.

In addition to sharing the stresses of running a still new business, and caring for Abbie and Carrie, Jane had embarked on another book of her own.

Through our dealings with SAMS we had met the redoubtable Alf Cooper and his wife Hilary. Hilary, with her two sisters and two brothers, children of SAMS missionaries, had toured Britain as the famous Los Picaflores harp and guitar group.[38] Alf had been brought up in Chile but attended school in England. Converted while at Bristol University, he had gone on to study at All Nations before joining SAMS. Alf and Hilary would plant a series of churches and missions in Santiago – fostering an evangelical witness in a strongly Catholic area – and in later years Alf (by now the Reverend Alfredo Cooper) would become chaplain to the President of Chile.

Alf, a cheerful, bold, and innovative leader, was full of spectacular stories, but no writer, so Jane bravely agreed to co-author an early autobiography. Published in 1993 as *It Shouldn't Happen to a Missionary*, with a cover by Taffy Davies and bolstered by Alf's reputation as a speaker and pioneer, it was very well received.

The missionary strand of our publishing remained important, and for a number of years Monarch served as the publishing partner for the Overseas Missionary Fellowship. OMF had developed from Hudson Taylor's famous China Inland Mission, after Mao threw the missionaries out of China. OMF was, and remains, a large, dynamic mission, and for decades it has had a strong publishing wing.

One day a chance enquiry about Hudson Taylor's biography, with which I had been involved at Hodders,

38. Los Picaflores: The Hummingbirds.

gave rise to a wider discussion with their very capable director of communications, Julia Cameron (in later years director of publishing for the Lausanne movement). Julia and I both loved books and enjoyed seeking out potential authors, and soon Monarch was publishing four or five books a year for OMF, some very good indeed.

Unquestionably the finest to emerge from this partnership was *Killing Fields, Living Fields* by OMF missionary Don Cormack. Cormack described, through the eyes of six representative Khmer families, the extraordinary sufferings undergone by the Christian church in Cambodia under the Khmer Rouge. The Khmer Rouge – the Communist Party of Kampuchea – ruled Cambodia between 1975 and 1979. Under their leader Pol Pot, they tortured and purged and murdered hundreds of thousands of ordinary citizens; many more died in the famines resulting from forced collectivisation (a policy under which peasant farmers were evicted from their individual holdings and required to join large collective farms). Any foreign connection – and Christianity was perceived as a Western intrusion – was ruthlessly eradicated. In the space of four terrible years the Cambodian genocide led to the death of 1.5 to 2 million people, around a quarter of Cambodia's population.

Julia asked me to take a look at the very long text: she was sure there was something there, but how could so diverse a book be contained in one set of covers? As I read, with mounting astonishment and streaming eyes, the title came to me, an obvious riff on the celebrated film *The Killing Fields*: once you have the title, a book often falls into focus, and so it proved.

Despite its length and hefty price tag, *Killing Fields, Living Fields* was a hit, dominating the Christian bestseller lists and selling tens of thousands. It received the accolade of CBC Book of the Year for 1997, and demonstrated beyond question that the term 'missionary' is not the kiss of death if you have the right book.

Alongside the books something else was happening.

In 1994 Edward England rang me. After leaving Hodders in 1980 he had set up first a profitable literary agency, Edward England Books, and then an independent publishing company, Highland Books, which had published Gordon MacDonald's phenomenally successful *Ordering Your Private World*.

A close friend of the distinguished author Michael Harper, Edward had also acquired – for a handshake and five pounds – the magazine *Renewal*, formerly the mouthpiece of The Fountain Trust. The Trust, set up by Michael in 1964 to promote awareness of the charismatic renewal and the exercise of spiritual gifts, had achieved great things, fostering dialogue across denominations and holding highly popular conferences. Remarkably and commendably, it closed its doors in 1980 at the height of its success, having achieved its primary objectives. At this point Edward stepped in, spotting a valuable mailing list and a community suddenly bereft of its principal organ of communication.

A decade later, *Renewal* was an established and prosperous magazine with a capable staff, operating out of Crowborough, a few miles to the south of our village. Edward had also started another magazine, *Healing and Wholeness*, based upon the magazine of the nearby Burrswood House of Healing.

Now he planned to retire. Would we like to take it all on – the agency, the books, the magazines, the dozen or so staff, the lease in Crowborough?

It was an extraordinary, and generous, opportunity. Monarch was doing relatively well, but we were constrained by lack of capital. While we stayed small, we would tick over nicely, but I didn't want to stay small.

Jane and I talked it through with Andrew Baines, a near neighbour and friend, who had enjoyed a distinguished Army career before setting up his own business consultancy. Rapier-thin, a gifted strategist, a Mensa member and a whizz with numbers, Andrew would play an indispensable part in our lives over the following few years, as would his wife Janet, a shrewd lady and our tax consultant. Together we looked at the business case, the workload, the agency's list of authors (which included George Carey, then Archbishop of Canterbury, and others of the country's most distinguished Christian leaders and writers). We considered the lease (on offices in Crowborough High Street). We met the staff.

I knew nothing about magazines, not all that much about running a business, and very little about being a literary agent. But I knew a good deal about the Christian community in Britain. And, at the back of all the questions and calculations, this seemed like an opportunity sent from heaven. Years earlier I had turned down a really good chance with Scripture Union; a year or two previously I had rejected attractive overtures from HarperCollins, because I was just setting up Monarch; this was the third plum to have come my way, and something inside said, 'This one.'

I rang Edward, and said, 'Yes.'

Fools rush in. Good grief, I had a lot to learn.

A book is a dialogue between reader and author, of which the writer hears only half. But, at base, just two people are involved.

Not so a magazine. A magazine serves a community. The editor seeks material representing a viewpoint. The adverts service the community's needs. The pages of Readers' Letters are pored over, applauded, dismissed, corrected, and contradicted.

This was the genius behind Edward England's acquisition of *Renewal*. The magazine we had acquired, ably edited by Wallace Boulton, an Anglican minister, carried stories drawn from the charismatic worldview – at its simplest, the strand of Christian faith holding that miracles did not end with the Book of Acts, but continue today; that the gifts of the Spirit may still be received, including gifts of healing, prophecy, and discernment; that speaking in tongues may be a regular aspect of a Christian's prayer life; that *renewal*, the baptism in the Holy Spirit, is an essential component of the Christian experience.

Charismatics, in this sense, are to be found in many parts of the Christian Church. Anglican and Catholic, Baptist and Methodist charismatics alike will say 'Amen' to the above. There may be disagreement over priesthood and sacraments and structures of authority, but the active, interventionist presence of the Holy Spirit is a common thread.

Michael Harper, David Watson, and other Christian leaders had pushed hard for this strand to be allowed a voice within the mainstream denominations, and had in large measure succeeded, often against strong opposition. As I have recounted, my own tentative exploration of the Anglican priesthood had come to an abrupt stop over the matter. It became for many believers a line in the sand. For years I chose to describe myself as an evangelical charismatic Anglican, a fairly standard brand of believer in the UK, but a source of sad confusion to my American friends, for whom evangelical and charismatic were as different as cheese and chocolate.

Renewal was the voice of this community. Each issue sought a balance across the denominations, telling stories and offering teaching about the charismatic understanding of the faith.

When in 1994 the Toronto Blessing broke upon the scene, a wave of revival with outbreaks of exuberant rejoicing, it was to *Renewal* that many turned for an authoritative account of the phenomenon. I first got wind of events in Toronto from an incautious journalist on a rival magazine, who was prematurely keen to rejoice at having scooped a story. I went into the office on a Saturday morning, called the printer to halt that month's issue, made urgent phone calls, and replaced Wallace Boulton's editorial with a quick account of the revival, which had started at the Toronto Airport Christian Fellowship.[39] Subsequent issues reported the wildfire spread of the Blessing, and in 1995 Wallace compiled a

---

39. Now Catch the Fire Toronto.

popular collection of these articles for Monarch, under the title *The Impact of Toronto*, which sold in thousands.

This was publishing! My first love was books, and to books I would return, but in a (largely) pre-internet era, to publish such a magazine was heady stuff, affirming a community, influencing opinion at the heart of thinking and decision-making.

There was another aspect. The economics of magazine publishing were far more attractive than the world of books. You were building a brand with every issue. You sold subscriptions, you sold copies through the shops, you sold advertising: three sources of revenue. It was labour-intensive, and the monthly wage bill was considerable, but with energy and focus the whole thing stayed on track. By comparison books required a lot of time, each book was an individual risk, and the payback was painfully slow.

Along with *Renewal* we had acquired *Healing and Wholeness*, edited by the distinguished theologian and Anglican priest John Gunstone. A quarterly publication, it sold far fewer copies, and struggled to establish blue water between its specialist focus and that of the more wide-ranging *Renewal*. When John decided it was time to retire, Jane leapt at the chance to edit it, and under her leadership it moved to a bi-monthly output and changed its title and focus to *Wholeness*.

Edward was a publisher of genius, but he did not greatly relish the world of computers, and when we took over his magazines, the office boasted one clunky but formidably expensive early beast of a machine, which used vast floppy disks to record subscribers. The production of the magazine was strictly analogue. Each month's issue was printed out, column by column, carefully cut up with scissors and pasted down with Cowgum, before being sent to the printers for scanning – black and white only, of course.[40] This was antiquity in motion, and we needed to catch up. For over a year I ploughed our profits into getting the office in Crowborough up to speed: mainly PCs, but a Mac for the designers. The team became used to unpacking yet another massive monitor, and a new line of expenditure – IT consultancy – appeared in the company accounts.

Alongside these new developments I was working hard to keep the output going for Monarch, publishing about thirty new books a year. Two magazines, a publishing imprint, and – not to be overlooked – a respectable literary agency, Edward England Books. Jane was carrying a good deal of weight, but the workload was phenomenal. We were responsible for paying ten people's wages and the pace was frenetic.

In addition, I had been licensed as a Reader in the Church of England, and was preaching several times a month in the three-church united parish.

Something had to give.

During the late 1980s and early 1990s, I became hooked on exercise. I had discovered regular workouts helped me think, and endorphins generate a glow which only athletes know. I was visiting the gym several times a week.

---

40. Cowgum made a regular appearance in the office overheads. For our designer's birthday a colleague made her a Cowgum-tin-shaped cake.

One evening I went out for a run, a three-mile course to the next village and back, a route I followed regularly, always trying to beat my own best. That night I felt a worrying pain behind my breastbone, and the following morning, without saying anything to Jane, I slipped along to the village surgery.

My doctor listened carefully to my chest, then told me to ring my wife, while he called an ambulance. Within forty-five minutes I was being processed through intensive care in Tunbridge Wells, with electrodes festooning my chest. I felt an immense fraud, and a bigger fool. Jane arrived half an hour later, alarmed but in control. Over the next few days, she held everything together while the medics prepared a diagnosis, and came with me a week or so later when I travelled up to St Thomas's Hospital in London for an angiogram, which revealed a blockage in one of the arteries close to my heart. The consultant nodded and scheduled me in for an angioplasty, where a stent (a small tube) is inserted in a blood vessel to increase flow. The incision is commonly made in the groin.

I was in some respects fit, but my stress levels had soared, and my cholesterol was too high. Our church prayed, hard. So did I. Running can reduce cholesterol, and I upped my regular jogs, covering more than fifteen miles a week over the steep local hills. I also turned my back on my dearly loved cheese. My father, a lover of fine cheeses,[41] had died of a heart attack at seventy-three, and my card was marked.[42]

---

41. One of his favourite sayings: 'What a *dommage*, we've got no *fromage*.' Sing hey for Frenglish.
42. I assumed at the time that dairy products were to blame, following the then widespread low-fat creed. These days I would pay more attention to sugar: see Gary Taubes, *The Case Against Sugar*, Portobello Books, 2018.

Six weeks later I returned to St Thomas's for my op. I was not looking forward to it. Edward had undergone similar treatment a few years earlier, and had spoken eloquently of the pain. In the operating theatre the electrical table hummed and turned beneath me while I watched my heart thumping away on a monitor. There were muttered discussions on the edge of my hearing. Then a beaming face appeared above me. 'You've cleared it,' the consultant informed me. 'The blockage has gone.'

I have rarely felt so much the need of a Presence to thank, and give thanks I did. It is one of the more genial arguments for the existence of the Almighty.

With care I was out of the woods, but the episode shook us. Clearly, I needed to change tack. But how?

A first stage was to sell the literary agency. It is just about impossible, I had discovered, to run a literary agency and a publishing house at the same time, because you want to reserve all the juicy titles for your own list. The agency was making decent money, but it demanded time and close attention; it was an easily separated element, and so we sold it.[43]

Then we took a long, hard look at the Monarch operation, and a harder look at the magazines. There was no question which of the two was earning our bread. We could ratchet back on the books, and focus on our two magazines, but simply reducing output felt like an intolerable limitation as my energy levels recovered.

---

43. We were unwise in our choice of buyer, as it turned out. The gentleman who purchased the agency fell on hard times, to put it mildly, and many authors lost large sums, among them my future wife Pen Wilcock.

How would it be, we wondered, if we were to start another magazine? Not a conventional approach to stress reduction, you might object, but the bubbling optimism that has led me into so many scrapes was strong upon me.

Two choices lay before me, and I made the wrong call.

One day John Paculabo, from Kingsway, asked if I would meet him for breakfast in London with Keith Danby, head of Send the Light. John and Keith were big guns, heavy hitters: they were both experienced businessmen and committed Christians.

Slightly bemused, I joined them early one morning in a plush hotel foyer.

Over toast and jam they set out their idea. The Christian book trade had seen several iterations of a trade magazine, but none had succeeded. Yet shops and publishers needed a voice and meeting place, and I knew the world of books: could I start a new magazine, with their backing and blessing?

I barely gave the idea the time of day. I pointed out that publishing budgets were being slashed, so advertising would be modest (and would drain revenue from our existing magazines); the subscriber base would be 2,000 at best; shops already had teams of sales reps hammering on their door, so were well up to date. Had I been even slightly prescient I would have added that the internet was set to steal the clothes off the back of traditional magazine publishing.

All these objections held water. And yet. The market for such a specialised publication remains, because the world of Christian books is a community in itself; the publisher would be in a position of considerable influence; the magazine, if competently handled, might augment the work of reps, if not supplant them; such a focused publication would attract more advertising support than any general magazine.

There is dumber, and there is dumbest. I turned John and Keith down.[44]

We called the new magazine *Celebrate*.

In preparation, we passed the production, financial, sales, and warehousing functions of Monarch Books to Angus Hudson Ltd in Mill Hill, north London, retaining the editorial aspects. Nick Jones, the owner and co-founder, had recently been joined by Rod Shepherd, who had been handling Monarch's design and production for some years, so it was a natural match. These new friendships would prove the only really excellent aspect to emerge from the next two years.

It had been Edward England's idea, several years previously, to start a magazine for the nation's Anglicans, and we thought it a good one. However, Edward had never actually got round to setting the wheels turning, a fact that should have given us pause.

I made a fundamental mistake at the outset, putting our money behind a dream rather than sober reality. That dream was the Church of England itself.

Our plan was to produce a magazine appealing to all strands of Anglicanism, from evangelical to high church.

---

44. Such a magazine did emerge. After various changes of names and owners, it is now flourishing as *Together* magazine, edited and published by the heroic Steve and Mandy Briars.

Jane, Andrew Baines, and I spent an informative afternoon in the office of the C of E's communications director, in Westminster, who must have been pleased that some wide-eyed enthusiasts were planning to make his job easier, and asking not a penny for the privilege. An energetic, voluble, strikingly profane American, he did all he could to assist us and make introductions, but the same flaw ran through his thinking as through Edward's original idea.

The flaw was this: the market for which we were publishing simply did not exist, beyond the minds of the central hierarchy.

I *knew* this. Christendom is wonderfully tribal, and within the straining brackets of the Church of England exist many tribes. The long debates over women's ministry and homosexuality provide ample evidence.

The matter revolves around authority. Evangelicals look to the Bible, and love answers. High church folk look to the priesthood and sacraments. Liberals, who serve at the altar of scholarship, concentrate on refining questions. This is offensively crude, and there are dozens of nuances, but in every English town these three principal strands will appear. It is dreadfully easy to trip over lines in the sand: over the place of women in leadership; over gays; over transgender issues; over remarriage of divorcees; over which version of the Bible to use; over which side of the altar to stand – and then, to add colour, there are strongly held local allegiances to do with the form of worship and the musical taste of the choir. The job of senior leadership is almost impossible: herding cats and tortoises.

Yet it was my home. The atheists might have nicked the lead off the roof, and the nursery given over to dust and spiders, but it's where I lived.

From a publisher's point of view the choice is simpler. Either you publish for the evangelicals, or you don't. Anglicans may all be one, in the eyes of God and the General Synod, but they don't read the same stuff or share the same heroes.

I am still angry, years later, at my own rose-tinted naivety. If we had set out our stall as a newsy, entertaining, and informative magazine for evangelical Anglicans, I think we would have succeeded, and I learned later that our plans badly worried the weekly *Church of England Newspaper*, which caters to that constituency. But I had bought too willingly into the vision of a journal for the national church, and it took two years and a great deal of money to confirm what I would have advised, had I been a consultant on the project: you have to see what *is* there, not what *ought* to be there.

We gave it our very best shot. We thought hard about design. We hired an excellent editor. We boosted our sales team and advertised the new publication everywhere we could afford, pouring in resources.

But the second issue, by my choice, contained an article by a leading member of the Lesbian and Gay Christian Movement – I was keen to publish for the whole body of faith – and what had been an encouraging flow of subscriptions fell abruptly away. Several congregations which had taken out group subscriptions asked for their money back. Advertising declined sharply (our initial issue had attracted nearly £20,000, but that was soon a fading memory).

We would soldier on for nearly two years, twisting and turning, commissioning good articles and photographs, seeking to be both inclusive and challenging. It was a waste of time. Too few trusted us: the liberals thought we were too evangelical; the evangelicals knew we were dodgy; the Anglo-Catholics found too little to their taste and ignored us.

We drained our other sources of income to keep the wagon on the road. We had taken on additional people to cope with the extra workload, but all too often the advertising staff had nothing to do. The day came when, to pay the print bill for *Renewal*, which was still trundling along healthily, we had to raise an additional mortgage on our house. I asked our building society for a cheque made payable to our printer. Andrew and I drove it down to Brighton and handed it over. I still remember driving away from that painful encounter, immediate relief warring with long-term despair.

Nick Jones, who came over one day for a chat, looked at me hard and quietly asked, 'Tony, is it time to quit?'

It was. *Celebrate* had achieved a circulation of about 3,500: had we made it to 4,000 the magazine would have reached break-even. We had thrown all we had at the venture, but the pump was dry. We were very weary.

I spent grim months in 1999 negotiating the break-up of our business. It was a horrible end to the millennium. We made most of the team redundant.[45] *Renewal* and *Wholeness* we sold to *Christianity* magazine, which was

---

45. Premier Radio, owners of *Christianity*, took on the lease in Crowborough and quickly rehired several members of staff. The link with Crowborough has continued, and Premier today has a substantial office in the town.

delighted to absorb its main rival.[46] *Celebrate* we sold to the *Church of England Newspaper*. Monarch Books we sold to Nick Jones, who treated us generously. And I started a daily ninety-minute run around the M25 to Mill Hill in north London, where I now joined the Angus Hudson staff. My long involvement with magazines was over.

It was a comprehensively ghastly time, yet I do not truly regret anything beyond my own dullness. We paid every bill, satisfied every creditor in full. Jane and I reckoned that, between the funds we had poured in and the assets we had lost, we had kissed goodbye to something approaching £250,000, but if we had succeeded, even modestly, we would have been wealthy, and the British Church would have had a wider choice of reading matter. *Christianity* magazine and the *Church of England Newspaper* emerged stronger for their acquisitions.

Monarch Books, which could easily have faded from sight, would survive and flourish under the umbrella of a larger concern.

---

46. For a while the merged magazine was called *Christianity and Renewal*, but that unwieldy moniker didn't endure.

10

Angus Hudson

A.A. Milne's *The House at Pooh Corner* is peopled with archetypes. Are you a Pooh or a Piglet, an Eeyore or a Kanga? A Rabbit, or – if suitably sage and venerable – a Wol? It was a game Jane and I had played, and I was unquestionably a Tigger (who always seems bigger, because of the bounces).[47]

Bouncing proved difficult, at least in those early days.

I had run my own company for the best part of a decade, and had been in charge of operations for sixteen years. Dancing to someone else's tune was hard to stomach. My decisions were no longer my own, my ideas required consultation. It felt frustrating and humiliating.

In other words, I was a sad pain to my new colleagues, who had the grace to work around my angularity. Rod Shepherd, positive and always cheerful, did a lot to ease the transition: he too had run his own business, and knew what it was like to cope with disappointment. A new editor, Eleanor Trotter, arrived in Mill Hill at much the same time, and proved an admirable fellow labourer, shrewd in judgement and more meticulous than I.

---

47. Jane oscillates between Eeyore and Kanga. As she acknowledges herself, she is hard to classify.

Eleanor and I formed the editorial team for the Monarch imprint; Rod's responsibilities ranged widely, but his special focus was design and print.

Nick, however, was the lynchpin. Nick had qualifications in both accountancy and art. In his youth he had played for the England hockey team; he had been a professional diver (in the aqualung sense); a huge and powerful man, he looked as if he could eat a billiard ball at every meal. He could be very tough and, in the days before his conversion to the Christian faith, had worked as a facilitator and path-clearer for Robert Maxwell at the British Printing Corporation. His inventiveness, ebullience, careful attention to detail, and generosity of spirit were legendary.

He and his wife Carol loved their golf, and I yielded to their unremitting enthusiasm, gradually discovering for myself why so many adore this eminently frustrating sport.

My arrival at Angus Hudson in the autumn of 1999 coincided with the launch of Dr John Stott's *The Birds Our Teachers*, released under their Candle imprint (which usually published books for children). Dr Stott, rector of All Souls, Langham Place, was not only a gifted Bible teacher and elder statesman in the evangelical wing of the Anglican Church; he was also a dedicated lifelong twitcher, whose camera skills furnished the illustrations for this unlikely but charming hardback. He had been writing the book for a decade or more, but Nick and Carol's personal enthusiasm and the company's reputation for beautiful books sealed the deal. Carol had placed a print order for several thousand, but on publication it quickly became clear that the book would far exceed expectations. Nick called the printers in Hong Kong and ordered further stock by air freight. Copies melted away as they hit the ground: everyone loved 'Uncle' John, and it made the finest Christmas gift imaginable.

Stott's genial bestseller dominated the foreground, but the arrival of the Monarch imprint changed the rhythm of life at Angus Hudson. Up to that point the international packaging aspect of the business had dominated proceedings – that is, the development of international co-editions, as I outlined earlier, where a large colour print run is built up, with each language on a separate black plate, so that the cost of artwork, design, and printing is spread across the whole. This means, for instance, that the unit cost of a smaller Welsh or Norwegian edition can be brought into line with the unit cost of a larger German or Spanish edition.

To organise such combined editions takes oodles of creativity, a fine eye for appropriate art, a lot of time, much patience, and a supernatural ability to network, and over the decades Nick and his team had built up a range of friendships with dozens of publishers across continents. Concurrently with this had developed the fantastically impressive Candle list, incisively managed by Carol, which focused on the retelling of Bible stories for children. Candle was often the British customer for the international operation, a very neat arrangement. Many of the books were printed in China, then shipped around the world, the multi-layered whole orchestrated from Mill Hill.

I knew the theory, but it was quite another thing to see it at close quarters. The books were simply so delightful. The book trade loved them. The turnover was astonishing to a man who dealt in paperbacks. Print runs of ten or thirty thousand, across a spectrum of languages, are a common feature of such publishing, and though profit percentages are modest, the actual numbers are jaw-dropping.

It's hard work, and requires sustained attention to detail. Books produced in this way require years to generate, but can stay in print for decades, selling sometimes in millions.

Paperbacks march to quite a different drum, and magazines shimmy along at ten times the speed of paperbacks. By temperament a darting soul, I wanted to sign up books and get them out into the market *now*.

But I had to ditch the habit of command. Years of calling the shots had left me lacking the grace of patience. The early months at Angus Hudson I spent in rebuilding my mental gearbox, amending the gearing ratio, working out how to corral my churning ideas to fit a longer time frame.

Simultaneously, the Monarch programme underwent a shift in emphasis. For its first twelve years or so Monarch had handled little in the way of biography, originally because it was one of Kingsway's strengths, but also because I had grown weary of biography at Hodders, where it was a mainstay of the religious list. Now Rod pushed me to consider whether we might not be missing a trick.

With the active assistance of literary agent Pieter Kwant we bought several really good biographies.[48] *Nobody's Child* by John Robinson described his transition from teenage rebel and petty criminal to brilliant youth worker: he and

---

48. For clarity, Pieter was not the gentleman to whom we had sold the Edward England agency.

his team drove a refitted double-decker through the tough sink estates around Manchester, offering youngsters mired in drugs, sex, and violence a chance to chat, play games, obtain advice, and discover a new perspective. The Manchester police loved John and the wider contribution of the Eden Bus Project and The Message Trust: where the bus went, crime rates fell, and they were glad to send some of their budget Eden's way.

Another remarkable story was that of Sokreaksa S. Himm, a Cambodian pastor who had escaped from the Khmer Rouge. Wounded but not killed by an execution squad, the boy hid under the corpses of his family before making his way to a camp on the Thai border and thence to Canada. Now a mature man, and a Christian believer, he had returned to Cambodia where, with the tenacity which had enabled his survival, he was establishing fellowship after fellowship. In a move of superlative grace, he had sought out the men who had executed his parents and siblings, and had led them to Christ. Reaksa told his story in *The Tears of My Soul*.

These two books sold in tens of thousands, and proved the start of a new emphasis for the Monarch list. But in 2001 Pieter sent me a book of an entirely different magnitude.

The Heavenly Man is the story of Brother Yun, a Chinese pastor who spent years on the run or in prison for his faith. A believer of great fervour, he lost no opportunity to proclaim the gospel, and was a wanted man in several provinces. Arrested and tortured by the authorities, he spent years in Hangzhou Maximum Security Prison before he seized an opportunity and simply walked out of the gates in obedience to the Holy Spirit, while guards at every checkpoint stared blankly through him. In due course he and his family found asylum in Germany, which is still his base.

This dry retelling does little justice to a complex and often heart-rending tale.

The Christian world has its share of charlatans, and plenty of folk with a strong will to believe. Part of the publisher's job in such circumstances is to exercise due diligence, and several aspects gave us pause. *The Heavenly Man* describes a seventy-four-day fast from food and water, for example, and there are many accounts of miracles. We were willing to acknowledge the miraculous at Angus Hudson, but only after appropriate scrutiny, and the story was hard to confirm. Author Paul Hattaway spoke fluent Mandarin and had travelled widely through China in the course of his research, so he seemed trustworthy, and Pieter vouched for him without hesitation. But we needed someone who could endorse Brother Yun himself. Salvation came in the substantial form of Stuart Windsor[49] of Christian Solidarity Worldwide, whom we trusted, and who had no hesitation in backing author and book. 'He's the real deal,' said Stuart, supporting his enthusiasm with a handsome order.

---

49. Stuart himself was among the more unusual people I have had the privilege to meet. The National Director of CSW for nineteen years, he worked incessantly in the cause of human freedom, and everyone who met him loved him. In the course of a distinguished career he gave evidence about persecution of Christians before both Houses of the US Congress; for the UN High Commissioner for Refugees; and during hearings of both the UK and European parliaments. A detail sticks in my memory, of the genial giant offering to buy me a snack in London's Regent Street, and greeting the short-order Asian chef behind the counter with immense enthusiasm, having previously befriended him and his family. A decade later I had the privilege of publishing his own excellent story, *God's Adventurer*. He died in 2017.

The book had an astonishing impact, selling over 750,000 in English alone and being translated into dozens of languages including Arabic and Mongolian. It was chosen as CBC Book of the Year in 2003. Yun, a humble man, is now an international evangelist.

But why did this particular book take wing, when others have not? Over the years I have published other titles with a similar impact – Peretti's *This Present Darkness* a notable example – which seemed to me to be strong books, and have taken off. Others, just as distinctive, just as well honed, have rolled idly from the cannon's mouth and come to rest behind the scenery. Perhaps it is timing; perhaps it is the idea; perhaps it is the author; perhaps it is a measure of quality. But there are no formulae. All you can do, as a publisher, is to endeavour to be alert to useful networks; to try to hear the deep hungers of your culture; to listen to the Spirit; to do your own job well; and to respond to enthusiasm, whether your own or others', with a warm heart and a cautious brain.

These books, and others, added significant turnover to the Angus Hudson account. Clearly, I had a role within the company, but to reach Mill Hill meant an arduous drive. Within a year Jane and I started to think about leaving Kent.

I had used the long trudge around the M25 to some effect, recording onto cassette the part of Thomas Becket, in Eliot's *Murder in the Cathedral*, and then learning the enormous quantity of lines – Becket has about a third of the entire text. I had proposed to our church, St Mary's Speldhurst, that we should mount a production of the play as our contribution to the various millennium celebrations, and our friend Sarah Knott, as director, assembled a team of aspiring thespians. We performed it over a couple of nights, to packed audiences, and were well pleased with the response.

But this aside, the three hours a day in the car proved wearisome, and with Carrie about to depart for university, the time was propitious for a move. Speldhurst had been our home for fifteen years, and we valued the many warm friendships, but thought we could land on our feet. After some bucketing around the towns north of London, we settled on Cheshunt. With the closure of the magazines Jane had thrown herself into the world of counselling, and had recently qualified: we chose a house with sufficient space for her to see clients privately.

Leaving Speldhurst was tough, and on the morning of our move we hugged one another and wept. Cheshunt represented a monumental change; a new set of friends; a new church; a new location, utterly unfamiliar.

Not long after we moved to Cheshunt in 2001, I joined the board at Angus Hudson.

One afternoon Nick invited me into his office for a quiet word. Out of the blue he had received a call from Lion Publishing in Oxford, suggesting a conversation about a possible merger.

11

Lion Hudson

Lion was started in 1971 by David and Pat Alexander. They had met when both served on the staff of InterVarsity Press, but both grew impatient with the limitations of the Christian market. Their vision was to generate Christian books for sale on the high street, books which would bear comparison, in content and presentation, with the best titles available from any publisher in the nation.

Their first publication was *A Pictorial Guide to the Holy Land*. Their second, in 1973, was *The Lion Handbook to the Bible*, a lavishly illustrated and wonderfully informative commentary on every book and chapter of the Bible, together with over a hundred accessible articles by reputable scholars. The Alexanders edited it themselves, and invested in it their resources and their souls. They called it 'the best book to have next to the Bible' – a fine piece of copywriting.

To publish such a volume was to climb a mountain. Simply to find, then negotiate permission to use, the hundreds of colour photographs required endless patience, phone call after letter after meeting. Maps and drawings had to be commissioned. The text from so many authors had to be harmonised, edited, brought to a common standard: all done on manual typewriters. There were endless sets of proofs. To print such an immense book was a challenge – many printers were cautious about the finances of the new company – and finally Angus Hudson himself stepped in to help organise the hefty initial print run.

A mine of information and insight, *The Lion Handbook to the Bible* caused a sensation. It was released while I was studying town planning at Nottingham University, and the university Christian Union gave over a weekly meeting to the *Handbook*, stacked feet deep beside the exit.

Now in its fifth edition, it has sold over three million copies and, despite its length, has been translated into dozens of languages.

Traditional publishers such as Edward England were amazed and bemused. Edward was invited to visit the Lion offices, and returned shaking his head. 'They don't have desks,' he reported. 'They have drawing boards.'

A stream of further admirable books followed, and David and Pat guided the company through nearly three eventful decades, until David's health forced him to retire: he died in 2002, aged sixty-four.

Now Paul Clifford, Lion's managing director, invited us to a conversation.

After some jockeying, and months of discussion, the fundamental good sense of a merger won the day. The two companies were compatible in terms of turnover and ethos. Lion had two imprints, Lion and Lion Children's; Angus Hudson had two imprints, Candle and Monarch.

The two Lion imprints focused on Christian books for the general market; the two Hudson imprints focused on Christian books for the Christian market. Both companies had an extensive co-editioning operation, with a range of complementary skills and contacts. Both were widely trusted. The two children's imprints dominated that important market. Together we were stronger. It *worked*.

Surprisingly, one of the most contentious matters – because it represented the difference in cultures – was the email address. Lion's preferred style was tcollins@lionhudson.com; Hudson's preference was tonyc@lionhudson.com. Lion was well organised, relatively cautious, formal; Hudson more seat of the pants, buccaneering, informal, sometimes boisterous. Nick won the email skirmish, against considerable resistance, but in many respects the Lion model prevailed.

Lion had the larger staff, so it made sense to close the Mill Hill office and move everyone to Oxford. The deal was signed at the end of 2004.

I was fully behind the plan, but for me there was a cost. Lion had three directors; Angus Hudson four. Equity in such matters is vital. I volunteered to step down, as the most recent member of the board.

The history of business is littered with failed mergers. That this one succeeded is due in large measure to the tremendous care and restraint shown by Nick Jones and Paul Clifford. They spent hour upon hour, thrashing through contentious issues and picking their way around awkward personalities, modelling patience and quietly knocking heads when necessary.

The formalities were over, but the outworking took years; it was almost a decade before the various editorial departments fully integrated. There were separate accounting systems, contracts, sales agreements, royalty rates, discounts: a vast body of small detail, and so much information to master about the various backlists (Lion was founded in 1971, Monarch in 1988, Angus Hudson in 1989: that's time enough to publish a *lot* of books). Any publishing house is surrounded by a dense network of relationships, each a priority to the individuals concerned. We all had to become overnight experts at a new, combined style of management, much of which was still evolving. We had to learn to trust, and sometimes to shut up.

For Monarch, which remained my particular responsibility, there was an additional challenge: we were just passing the peak of the long success of *The Heavenly Man*, which slowly began to decline shortly after the merger took effect. The result was that Monarch posted falling sales month after month, and I had to point out to my worried colleagues that revenues – apart from Brother Yun – were increasing sharply.

A publishing axiom: a publisher is rarely so vulnerable as in the wake of a major success. You have seen income soar, and few publishers will simply stash the loot and wait for things to return to normal. Overheads increase, new staff get taken on, a raft of new titles signed. But unless the rising graph of costs stays within fingertip of the falling graph of revenue, you are for the high jump.

We knew this, and were cautious.

It had been over ten years since Monarch had published Neil Anderson's *Victory Over the Darkness* and *The Bondage Breaker*. Dr Anderson was prolific and diligent, and other volumes followed.

Just as the merger was taking place, we launched, with considerable trepidation, the Freedom in Christ Discipleship Course, a thirteen-week course for popular use, devised by Steve Goss and based on Neil's two main books.

Neil was a true intellectual, a good teacher, but his writing could be dense, tinged as it was by his years in the academic world. Steve, a successful businessman, astutely saw through to the core of Neil's message and created an accessible course intended for (but not limited to) new disciples.

Neil had founded Freedom in Christ Ministries in 1989, in the States. By this point it was a well-established organisation with branches in many parts of North America. But Steve Goss and his team – he set up the UK office in late 1999 – brought a new energy.

The premise of the course was this: churches have made many converts, but too few real disciples. Frequently new believers struggle to take hold of basic biblical truth and live it out, and often take a painfully long time to mature. This is not so much because churches lack resources or teaching, but rather because we all struggle to connect, genuinely and personally, with truth.

This is where the Freedom in Christ Course comes in. As we have seen, it is specifically designed to help Christians grasp who they are in Christ, resolve personal and spiritual conflicts through genuine repentance, and move on to maturity.

The Freedom in Christ Course, like the Alpha Course, is intended to be followed on a weekly basis, with an Away Weekend – again, like Alpha – part way through. It allows participants, in small groups, to examine, safely and without confrontation, every aspect of their lives and to assist one another as they move towards greater clarity and commitment. The underlying objective is the renewing of every part of the disciple's nature in Christ: helping believers to move on from the threshold and deeper into the Kingdom.

Steve and I agreed the course would work well as a follow-on to the Alpha Course established by Holy Trinity Brompton. Graduates of Alpha would be comfortable in each other's company, and used to studying together. We set up an appointment with Tricia Neill, executive director of Alpha International, who met us in the sunlit grounds of HTB. Would it be ok, we asked, if we could present Freedom in Christ as a natural next step to Alpha?

Tricia, an experienced and capable lady, looked at us carefully and rather severely: any successful leader must be aware of imitators, freeloaders, and piggy-backers.

'I hope you aren't going to imply that Alpha endorses your course?' she enquired.

We hastily assured her nothing was further from our thoughts (which was completely true: we just wanted to be open with her about what we had in mind).

'You're not planning to use the Alpha logo?'

No, certainly not.

'Ok, then. We're happy for you to go ahead. God bless your next steps.'

Walking away, Steve and I grinned at one another. An important door had opened.

The Freedom in Christ Course launched in October 2004, with a massive leader's guide containing the full text of the course (plus a CD-Rom containing slides and display material); a *Participant's Guide*, with space for notes, to make the book your own; a separate *Steps to Freedom in Christ* book for use on the Away Weekend; all accompanied by a full set of presentations by Steve Goss on several DVDs.[50] It represented years of work by Steve and his colleagues, and a significant manufacturing commitment. The full course wasn't cheap, either: a participating church of any size would need to invest hundreds of pounds.

You cannot launch such a course half-heartedly, but this was scarcely bookshop material, and no account was going to carry the range in depth. We devised a scheme to allow shops to act as conduits rather than stockists, but would it work? It was complicated to sell: would the Lion Hudson sales team cope? How could we publicise it? There are Christian courses aplenty, mostly less demanding and less expensive: what could crack the benign indifference which the market commonly displays to a publisher's enthusiasm? Would Steve's thousands of hours of effort pay off? Would we recoup our investment? None of us had ever tried to set up anything of the kind.

Rod Shepherd courageously signed off on the substantial outlay.

That the course found an audience is due entirely to the tireless commitment from Steve, his wife Zoë, and their little team to spreading the word. They adopted the

---

50. The DVDs featured Steve heavily: they were essentially filmed seminars. They turned him into a minor celebrity, and to his consternation he found himself being greeted enthusiastically by strangers in the street.

strategy of gathering together church leaders to offer, for a nominal charge, a day's Introduction to Freedom in Christ. These days proved popular, and sowed the seed.

It worked, magnificently. As of 2021 over half a million adults in the UK have gone through the course, and FICM have established national offices in nearly thirty countries, with Steve as International Director.[51] The impact of Neil Anderson's insights continues to spread.[52]

With the merger came a personal move, facilitated by a relocation grant from Lion Hudson.

I had spotted an opportunity. For decades I had cherished the idea of planting my own forest, buying some land and establishing a woodland as a heritage project. I wanted to call it Peter's Wood, after my father, a keen amateur naturalist.

It would have made better sense to find a house in Oxford, but a decent residence in the Oxford area with acres of land was beyond our budget. As a compromise, in 2004 we found a house in Bierton, just outside the market town of Aylesbury, about twenty-five miles from the Lion Hudson offices. The large bungalow we chose was devoid of character or architectural charm, but it did come with three acres of farmland, a double garage and a large garden.

---

51. Steve comments, 'I think it's fair to say that we've lost track of the figures.'
52. In the spring of 2021 Steve told me: 'We're currently partnering with a Hong Kong-based ministry who are well on their way to their target of getting a million copies of the course in Simplified Chinese into the underground church in China by way of putting it on SD cards for mobile phones.'

It was not her dream, but Jane acquiesced. She had accepted a demanding job as manager of a Relate centre in north London, overseeing seventy counsellors as well as other staff, and several charity shops. The drive in from Aylesbury was daunting, so she bought a flat near her office, staying there midweek and returning for weekends.

Carrie, meanwhile, had completed a degree in psychology and art for public space at the University of Roehampton: as part of her final portfolio, she undertook to decorate Jane's Relate centre with appropriate photos on the theme of togetherness. Togetherness would also be part of her own future, as during her final year she hooked up with Dan Raymond, younger brother of her closest friend Laurie. Dan was studying computer science in Brighton, and Carrie found delight in preparing meals for Dan and his flatmates at weekends. Today – married to Dan, with two flourishing sons – she is a professional cake maker in West Sussex, creating confections for all occasions. A most appropriate expression of psychology and art for public space.

Abbie had completed her schooling (she had attended several schools for those with special educational needs) and was now living with us in Aylesbury. Her health was and remains indifferent, but the long years of plaster casts were behind her. However, the relative backwater of Bierton was no place for a young woman, and Abbie felt isolated and bored. We decided to buy a house for her on an estate in Bedgrove, closer to the centre of Aylesbury, which she could share with lodgers: a measure of independence, but in range of help if needed.

I focused my spare energy on creating Peter's Wood in the meadow attached to our house. After taking soundings with local conservation bodies, I determined that the primary species of tree should be black poplar, a nationally scarce variety but relatively well established in Aylesbury Vale. The call went out to friends, colleagues, and family, and one spring morning about sixty people converged on Bierton armed with wellies and spades, and set to work, digging slots in the heavy clay and planting poplar cuttings, each protected by a horticultural tube. Others of the team focused on establishing the protective perimeter hedge of blackthorn, hawthorn, wild rose, and field maple. We fed the workers pizza and beer, and exhausted bodies littered our floors that night. A hard weekend of intense labour, and the wood was begun.

It should have worked. We had taken advice and carefully followed instructions. But the spring of 2005 was desperately dry, and it was beyond our capacity to water acres of baby trees. It was heart-breaking to watch as the rains failed and one by one the hundreds of little saplings broke into leaf, withered and died. The hedging plants – rooted, so less vulnerable to drought – weathered the conditions far better, and today the large field (for so it remains) has a respectable boundary of local trees.

Looking back, it is tempting to see the failure of Peter's Wood as a metaphor for the failure of my first marriage.

Jane and I had been struggling for years, and several times had sought counselling. Her intermittent depression, exacerbated by what she subsequently discovered to be late-onset Type 1 diabetes, was a steady burden upon her. She couldn't rely on her health, and her energy levels fluctuated wildly. I, meanwhile, caught up in the adventure of a new publishing initiative, was pouring all I had to offer into my work and into plans for the wood, and was less and less available. During the week we were apart. The Relate office was financially a fragile enterprise, and Jane was doing all she could to set it on a sound footing. She was making a new circle of friends at her place of work, and more and more frequently elected not to come home at weekends. When we did get together the strain was obvious. Our marriage had lasted over three decades, but was slowly disintegrating.

Both girls were launched on their adult lives.

In December 2005 we agreed to separate. I later married Pen Wilcock, by then a friend of many years' standing.

Despite this private crisis the world of books rolled on. As 2005 drew to a close, Christine Chouler appeared at my elbow.

Christine and her husband Roger, a talented designer, had been part of the Angus Hudson team for some years. I'd met Roger, a South African, at a mutual friend's wedding in the 1970s, and had given him one of his earliest commissions. The couple regularly returned to South Africa to see family.

Now Christine plonked a paperback on my desk. 'If you don't publish this, I'll never speak to you again,' she informed me. She was grinning, but very focused. 'It's a wonderful story,' she insisted. 'I couldn't stop reading. It'll make your head spin.'

The book was *Faith Like Potatoes* by Angus Buchan.

Angus Buchan, a farmer of Scottish extraction, had been a driven, hard-working, hard-drinking man, short of fuse and altogether too quick with his fists. Angus and his wife Jill established their first farm in Zambia, but to stay in Zambia would have meant sending their children away to school. So Angus moved his pregnant wife and three children to KwaZulu Natal in the south-east corner of South Africa, where he bought a plot of land and started to carve a viable farm out of the bush. Days were filled with backbreaking labour; evenings he spent constructing the family's homestead, while Jill struggled to cope in their one-room trailer.

The farm grew, but so did Angus's stress: his fast-ignited temper flared more and more easily. Jill was a firm Christian, but Angus had no time for faith – right up to the point where he finally went to church with his wife, and was profoundly converted.

Drought threatened the young enterprise, and Angus asked God for advice. 'Plant potatoes,' came the response. *Potatoes?* Potatoes are a famously thirsty crop: surely the new Christian was mistaken? Angus prayed again. 'Plant potatoes,' insisted the Lord.

Swallowing hard, Angus obeyed, investing his modest resources. His neighbours muttered and mocked, but the stubborn Scotsman would not be deflected – and was rewarded with a handsome crop which sold at premium prices.

Angus turned to the Lord to give thanks, but the Lord had a further instruction: 'Preach the gospel.' Angus had no experience as a public speaker, and his biblical knowledge was not yet well rooted: again, surely he had misheard? In trepidation he booked a small venue.

So started a massive international ministry, filling some of the largest stadia in Africa, where Angus focused on reaching men with the message of the gospel. Firemen and salesmen, executives and engineers turned to Christ in their thousands, won over by the plain-spoken farmer with the incandescent faith.

I loved the story, but the first edition (ghosted by a capable lady called Val Waldeck) was written very much from a South African perspective, with assumptions about attitudes and customs which muted its impact for a wider readership. The narrative needed fleshing out, and translating. After getting permission from Angus, I called in Jan Greenough.

Jan was, and is, a long-time friend, godmother to Abbie, and a skilled and capable co-author who had worked with me on a number of projects. But she had never been to South Africa: how could she bridge the gap?

The answer lay, as so often, in diligence, patient research, and imagination. One international phone call followed another. Jan sent Angus lists of questions, to which he would respond by the hour, mailing a succession of mini-cassettes to Oxfordshire for transcription. Jan is a lady of profound faith, but she couldn't let Angus off the hook. When God spoke, how did Angus hear? What did he make of the healings that had followed his rallies? His views on the roles of men and women were controversial: why had he said what he did? Why were hard-bitten builders, mechanics, and businessmen responding so eagerly? It might be a move of the Spirit, but what did that mean?

Angus, a humble man slightly stunned by his expanding ministry, responded patiently and carefully.

The new, expanded version of *Faith Like Potatoes* did respectably in the UK and US, but in South Africa it flew, especially after a film of Angus's story was released. Our South African distributor was startled, then astonished, as sales climbed and passed six figures.

The credit must go to Christine Chouler, who knew a good book when she saw one.

12

Second Intermission: MAI

In 2004 I first brushed shoulders, through Rod Shepherd, with the impressive undertaking that is Media Associates International. An experienced publisher, Bob Reekie, founded MAI in 1985 with two colleagues, Jim Johnson and Jim Engel. The three were determined to tackle a problem.

As I had discovered early in my career, American, and to a lesser degree, British Christian books dominate the skyline of the Christian world. Despite the fact that much of the Church's growth, youth, enterprise, and energy emanate from Africa, Asia, and Latin America, the vast majority of Christian books still emerge from the rich, Western and above all English-speaking nations. The vitality and scholarship that increasingly characterise the congregations of the developing world are not reflected in the literature the newly faithful read.

Bob and the two Jims wanted to see books written and published which reflected local cultures.

Some training was available for local writers, but writers need editors and publishers, and publishing needs a sound business footing. Bob and his colleagues shared a dream of an agency which could foster the appropriate skills, training local Christians in writing, editing, graphics, marketing, finance, management, sales, and production – in other words, the composite abilities required to make a success of a publishing company.

Their vision has been magnificently fulfilled. Since its inception MAI has trained over 10,000 people, on five continents, and in ninety countries. My colleague Rod Shepherd had founded the European branch.

One day in 2004 Rod stopped by my desk to ask if he could give my name to John Maust, president of MAI. A couple of days later the phone rang, and a gentle but incisive American voice explained what was at issue. They wanted to run a training course in Benin, in West Africa, John outlined, but the course needed to be presented in French. Might I be interested?

After he had hung up, I turned to my computer: to my embarrassment I had no idea where Benin might be. A long, narrow country on the south coast of West Africa, and formerly known as Dahomey, Benin is home to nearly twelve million people, and was once a centre of transatlantic slaving, the kings of Dahomey finding the trade a profitable outlet for surplus war captives. The official language is French, a legacy of its years as a colony. Benin gained independence from France in 1960, and after years of turbulence established a republic in 1990.

Now a group of local Christian leaders had approached MAI to ask if they might send a trainer. If someone could be found to provide a few days' teaching, they would undertake to gather a group of students.

After a certain amount of pondering – my French had grown rusty – I accepted the challenge.

A flurry of preparation followed as I concocted a basic introduction to the publishing world. I had no idea of the experience, competence or indeed the level of education, of those I would be teaching, and John could shed little light, as this was the first course to be held in Benin and the first time MAI had worked with the group there. Not only was I working blind, but there were all kinds of terms which needed translating: copyright law; production schedules; marketing priorities; design parameters; footnotes; permissions; so much more. What did people read in Benin? (*Did* they read? Literacy rates were low.) What did they do for entertainment, or was that a stupid question to ask people struggling to make ends meet?

In addition to preparing the course I needed tropical clothing, inoculations, and a visa. MAI booked a ticket for me (via Paris: there were no direct flights from the UK to Benin).

Stiff after the long journey, the passengers emerged blinking onto the hot concrete of Cotonou Airport. Shuffling through customs, I was relieved to be met by John Maust himself, a tall, thin individual who stood out from the milling crowds of returning Béninois. Grabbing my bag, John urged me through the throng and out into the African night, where waited a powerful four-wheel drive Toyota with a local pastor at the wheel. In short order we arrived at the church where the course would be held, and after unpacking, I joined John and our host for a late supper.

To my relief I could follow the local French well enough – rather more easily than John, whose second language is

Spanish – but with a sudden frisson of unease, I suddenly realised what our host was telling me: that the forty students who had assembled were not publishers, but booksellers. Would that be a problem?

It was Saturday night. Come Monday morning, I would be presenting the first session of a two-day course, in French, and my carefully prepared notes were almost entirely irrelevant.

Scanning the week's schedule, I saw with increasing horror that I had over fourteen hours of teaching to provide, and more than forty people to inform, stimulate, and entertain.

Decades back I had been a sales rep, and I'd kept in touch with various bookselling friends. I could make generalisations about book categories and knowing your customer, matters about which those attending the course could speak with far greater understanding.

What could I possibly offer them?

On Sunday morning I excused myself from the morning service and retired to my room, sifting through my notes for crumbs of useful wisdom, searching for common ground, and with desperate focus rewriting – in French – exercises and discussion topics. What sorts of books were they asked for? What did they know about local reading habits? Who were their customers' favourite authors?[53] Which were the peak selling times? Did they use colporteurs (peripatetic sellers of devotional literature)? Who were the local influencers? Could they work more closely with local pastors? How could they expand their

---

53. White American preachers, without exception. MAI was badly needed.

customer base? Did they go into local schools? How did they design their displays? Which covers worked? Did they know producers on their local radio station: could they get a regular slot to review new books? Was there a local paper which would welcome a column?

I realised I was scrabbling blindly, asking questions which might be entirely irrelevant. That night I slept badly.

The first day went tolerably well. The group, mostly men of middle years, were willing to be interested by the performing seal in their midst, and plied me with incisive questions. My halting French just about held up.

By the afternoon of the second day my audience was drifting off to sleep in the hot and crowded room. By three pm I ran utterly dry, apologised to my students, and slumped back into my seat.

At which point the leader of the event, a distinguished elderly gentleman, stood up and embarked on a vote of thanks. 'Mon cher Monsieur Tony . . . we thank you with the greatest possible sincerity . . . such eloquence . . . such a privilege to share in your extensive experience . . . you have given us so much to think about . . . to come such a distance . . .'

By my own estimation the past two days had merited a kindly nod, at best. On and on his speech rolled, orotund and flowery. Five minutes. Ten. Twenty. My polite smile started to go into spasm.

Then there was a disturbance at the back of the hall, and a man bearing an enormous, gift-wrapped box made his way down the aisle between the desks. Our host elegantly wound up his peroration, and held out the box to me with a broad smile. At his gesture I tore off the wrapping and opened the lid.

It was a suit of clothes, an African suit in sky blue. I shrugged into the jacket, which fitted perfectly.

The men of Benin dress magnificently. In central London they would stand out like flares. The most vivid colours, the sharpest cut: greens and purples, scarlets and yellows. As our host explained, he had invited a distinguished local tailor into the morning session the previous day, and the skilled gentleman – the box-bringer smiled – had measured me by eye from the back of the room, and set to work. My new suit was the result.

I was impressed, and overwhelmed. Back in England I would look a prize ninny if I attempted to wear it, but on the streets of Cotonou I fitted right in, apart from my face. For the next few days I had little to do, so sauntered proudly around the neighbourhood, ageing peacock that I was.

Thus began a series of adventures under the MAI banner. Over subsequent years I would carry my briefcase and flash drive to Mali, the Republic of Congo, Kenya, Italy, Lebanon, Russia, and Burkina Faso. Sometimes I would be speaking to writers, more often to booksellers, occasionally to publishers. After that first nerve-wracking trip the background briefings became more detailed, and my presentations gradually grew more polished.

Most readers of this book will have become accustomed to buying online, and easy access to the world marketplace is a given.

In many of the countries I visited, especially in Africa, this is not yet true, though the situation is changing rapidly. Fragile and sometimes corrupt postal services, limited access to online banking, political instability, and degraded infrastructure present a challenge even to international firms such as Amazon. Dr Jules Ouoba, head of Centre de Publications Evangéliques in Côte d'Ivoire, explained to me that if he wanted to send books to, say, the neighbouring country of Mali, he would probably have to mail them via *Paris* if there was to be a reasonable chance that they would arrive.

Accordingly, online retailing has not diminished the role of the traditional bookseller in most of Africa. To be a bookseller, as should be the case, is to be a valued member of the community, with access to cherished information, whose advice is sought when investing scarce resources in precious books. It's always a tough job, but in most of the countries I visited there are multiple additional challenges – sourcing and paying for books, obviously, and discerning what will be of use, but also exercising discretion when offered glossy American goodies from well-funded ministries; pricing books at a level where customers can both eat and read; protecting stock from heat, insects, dust, and damp; preventing rampant pilfering.

MAI is a well-established group, encouraging competent administration and good recruitment from its local organisers. In Brazzaville, in the Republic of Congo, the literature course was overseen, as often in West Africa, by Jules Ouoba whom I mentioned above, a burly, shrewd, candid gentleman who had gained his doctorate from the University of Bordeaux. Under his capable leadership the courses attracted talent, and I was struck forcibly, again and again, by the sheer calibre of the students. Sharp-witted, questioning, highly educated, articulate, filled with passion to play their part in transforming lives through Christian books: they were a pleasure to teach. The class in Brazzaville included two university professors and the head of Scouting for the whole country. All three yearned to run Christian bookshops.

Simply to reach the course could be a test of endurance. I was startled to listen to the account from another of my students of how he and two classmates had slept in their car for three nights as they made their way across country – to save money, obviously, but also to prevent their precious transport from getting nicked. And there were other trials. We had to move from the original venue because of the distress of one of the participants: Brazzaville had been the scene of violent conflict in an insurrection a few years previously (I was shown the bullet holes peppering buildings in the city centre) and one of the students had lost family members during fighting at our intended location.

In Brazzaville I was invited to tour the offices of a local Christian newspaper, and spent several hours with its editor and owner, drawing upon my years with *Renewal* magazine to comment on layout, editorial policy, and the advisability of a letters page. I was struck by the central double-page spread given over to a report, in minute detail, of the monthly giving by each of the denomination's churches. It seemed to me to be tedious beyond description, and I suggested alternatives. The editor grinned. 'It's the first thing our readers turn to,' he explained. 'Competition between churches is intense. It's a matter of pride to be at the top of the list.' Local knowledge is king.

As I left the offices he paused for a moment and gestured to a bulky old computer perched on a top shelf. 'When the revolution started, we knew these offices might be looted,' he told me. 'So we loaded our records onto the hard drive, wrapped it in plastic and buried it in the back yard. When, months later, the fighting died away, we found as we had expected that the whole place had been ransacked. Every machine, every chair, every shred of paper, all gone. But we dug up our computer and used it to start again.' He smiled. 'We call it Lazarus.'

The course in Bamako, in Mali, was also organised by Jules, and attracted participants from nine West African nations.

Mali's crowded streets are filled with motorcycles, often carrying three or four passengers. Life is lived in the open: each roadside is crammed with tiny booths selling radios, or water, or fruit. Every intersection is thronged with small boys selling phone cards and dancing amongst the moving traffic to wash windscreens.

'Mali' means 'hippo' and the capital, Bamako, means 'crocodile tail'. The city is bisected by the vast River Niger, which flows for 4,000km through that part of Africa and is used by the local inhabitants for washing, drinking, fishing and waste disposal.

The slogan 'One people, one faith, one law' was everywhere. The faith (and law) in question is Islam, to which ninety per cent of Malians adhere: nine per cent are Animist, and of the remaining one per cent, two-thirds are Catholic, so this is not promising territory for an evangelical Christian bookshop. Nevertheless, one exists, maintained by a local church. In a good week they may sell fifteen books. In practice there is a fair freedom of religion: an evangelist from one of London's black churches was running a very loud healing crusade in one of the city's parks. I formed the impression that Christians were so scarce as to offer little challenge to the authorities. In most other countries of the region Christianity and Islam are more evenly balanced.

Bamako stands out in my memory for being, above all, hot: well over forty degrees at its peak. Accordingly the courses started early in the morning, stopped for two hours at midday, then continued through the long, sultry afternoons.

We were meeting in a conference centre on the banks of the Niger, and during the lunch breaks we would sit beneath the waterside avocado trees, which threw ripe fruit at us. The classroom quickly resembled an oven. After a couple of days, my students and I decided to escape the corrugated iron roof of our meeting room and carried our chairs outside. It was the start of the rainy season, and as the day ended, you could watch the approaching storm fronts rolling across the river plain. In the evenings, after the intense downpour had eased, large frogs and larger toads would make their way up from the river to squat beneath the compound's lights, enjoying the rain of stunned insects. One afternoon I made the acquaintance of a praying mantis, and during the heat of the day was diverted by the large darting lizards in improbable bands of blue, white, black, and orange. Above the compound where we stayed, bats the size of pigeons flocked each evening. 'Back home we eat them,' said Jules.

On this occasion there were three trainers. Greg Burgess, an American living in France, who runs Editions Clé in Lyon, taught a band of editors, while the writing seminar was led by Lawrence Darmani from Ghana, who runs his own (English-language) publishing house, Step Publications. During the week each of the thirty students on his course was required to write a chapter on a matter pertaining to Africa's youth. CPE planned to publish the resulting books, an important boost to the young writers.

The week was not without its trials, and my luggage arrived forty-eight hours late. Fortunately I had packed my notes in my briefcase, and Lawrence kindly lent me a couple of shirts. When I emerged blinking the morning following our arrival, Jules – a man of decisive action – had already nipped out to the local market to buy me a packet of disposable razors.

My own twenty students were for the most part already running Christian bookshops. This is no small achievement in a region where you may have to wait months for stock, where functional literacy is low, and where local disapproval may result in your shop being burned to the ground. These men (plus one very accomplished lady) were motivated, brave, intelligent, passionate, and resourceful. During the course of the week we covered many of the usual aspects of the world of marketing – developing a customer base, understanding local needs, working with opinion formers, looking for sales opportunities, setting a budget, managing events, and so forth. We enjoyed a field trip to the best general bookshop in Mali (friendly but chaotic) and to the one Christian store which, despite slender resources, was far better managed – just as well, as the manager was attending the course. I set them a project aiming to improve their shops' performances, and received some truly imaginative proposals. The prize was won by a gentleman who already had Master's degrees in sociology and theology. His presentation left me optimistic about the future of Christian bookselling in Guinea.

Before I left Mali, I had personal business to attend to.

Pen's daughters are all intensely musical, and own a fine collection of instruments. Pen had asked me to get hold of a 'thumb piano' for my stepdaughter Alice. The kalimba, or thumb piano, originates in Africa. As I discovered far too late, it is basically a small box with a sound hole, to which are strapped metal strips of varying lengths, which when plucked emit a note. It's simple, robust, and portable. Did I mention that it is quite small?

Not for the first time in my life I assumed I had understood: an African instrument, played with the thumbs.

As the course wound to its conclusion, I mentioned to Jules that I might need his assistance in fulfilling my commission. When I described what I wanted, waggling my thumbs, he nodded. 'You mean a kora,' he told me. 'It's a traditional Malian instrument.'

That sounded about right.

The kora sits somewhere in the canon of stringed instruments between a lute and a harp. A large calabash, halved, is covered with cow skin to make a resonator. A long neck is attached, with two prongs on which the hands rest, jutting from either side of the base. The neck carries twenty-one strings, appropriately tuned and supported by a freestanding bridge. The substantial instrument, about four-feet tall, is held upright on the musician's lap, facing the player, and the strings are plucked with the thumbs and forefingers.

Jules organised an excursion to the local market, a vast sea of booths and alleys, selling all manner of foodstuffs, medicines, decorations, tools, clothes, weapons, and skins, redolent with scents and stinks. The air was full of bustle and noise, and Jules advised me to stay close as he surged through the morass of people, occasionally stopping to ask for directions.

Some hundreds of yards into the site, and just past a busy mosque, we came upon a circle of booths selling drums, guitars, pipes, and a wide selection of koras. The vendors turned as one, seeing a succulent potential customer, and a white, bewildered-looking customer at that.

How to choose among the many fine instruments on display?

Jules took control, facing down an insistent young man and insisting on obtaining advice. Muttering, the youth admitted defeat and turned down a path between the booths, summoning us to follow. Behind the stalls lay a small grassy area where a gentleman in elegant blue silk robes was sitting on a plastic chair, a finely made kora at his side. Jules politely explained our mission, and the musician sprang to his feet. Leading us back to the booths, he reviewed first one kora, then another, cocking his head, strumming a few notes, explaining in rapid-fire French why each was inadequate. Finally, one of the vendors disappeared into the back of his stall and emerged clutching a beautifully fashioned instrument. Our guide settled the kora upon his lap and played a few resonant riffs, then nodded. 'That one's got a nice tone,' he announced. Beaming, Jules told me to produce my dollars.

On the flight home there was no way that the kora, bulky and delicate, would fit into the Air France luggage rack, but the helpful crew secured it in their own locker space. In Paris, as I waited for my connection, I fielded a succession of queries. Could I play it? What was it called? When was my next concert? At London Airport the amused customs official waved me through. In the train it required a seat of its own.

When I opened our front door in Aylesbury, Pen looked stunned as I proudly lugged the kora into our hall. 'What on earth is that?' she asked in bewilderment.

The postscript to this story is that Pen and Alice took the kora down to London, where they found a home for it at a centre for the rehabilitation of the victims of torture. Many of those being treated were from West Africa, and the staff were delighted to receive such a gift.

13

Adventures in Storytelling

The new, blended publisher, Lion Hudson plc, dominated the market for Christian children's books, as everyone had hoped. Our commanding position, as publishers of both Lion Children's Books and Candle Books, gave us space to be truly creative. Nick Jones, deputy MD but entrepreneur-in-chief, was never happier than when leaning over a designer's shoulder. He was adamant that if you could stick an ISBN on it, it was a book. At one point he mooted a range of 'Holy Spirit' kites: we thought he was joking, but weren't sure. (Another idea which didn't see the light of day was a series of stained-glass jigsaws for the cathedral bookshop market.) Among hundreds of other projects, Nick and his crew produced a board game based on *The Pilgrim's Progress*, and worked closely with our design department to generate a handsome fold-out Noah's Ark, a triumph of complex paper engineering. Such products are costly to design and hugely expensive to manufacture, but both succeeded.

Meanwhile Lois Rock, *grande dame* of the Lion Children's division, continued to publish a formidable range of beautiful, classy volumes. Nick and Lois between them kept our team of designers hopping.

Dave Hill and Dennis Hillman, respectively the sales director and editorial director of our North American partners Kregel, relished the diverse output of the two children's imprints.

Early in our ownership of Monarch, as I have recounted, I had tried publishing fiction, not for the first time, and had discovered afresh how tricky it can be.

I love fiction, and usually have a novel on the go: it is not uncommon for me to read two or three a week. An American agent of my acquaintance calls it mind candy, and he's absolutely right, but a good novel provides nutrition as well as sweetness.

The impacts of *This Present Darkness* and *Piercing the Darkness* were still vivid in my mind. Despite my past failures in this sector, I wanted to publish more.

I believe, deeply, in the power of story. Fiction is a fine vehicle for truth. Story can get behind defences and disarm criticism. C.S. Lewis, author of the Narnia Chronicles, was asked by the founding editor of *Christianity Today*, Carl F.H. Henry, to contribute an article to the magazine's first issue, but refused, observing:

> My thought and talent (such as they are) now flow in different, though I trust not less Christian, channels, and I do not think I am at all likely to write more directly theological pieces . . . If I am now good for anything it is for catching the reader unawares—thro' fiction and symbol. I have done what I could in the way of frontal attacks, but I now feel quite sure those days are over.[54]

---

54. Quoted in *Christianity Today*, 27 December 2012

The critical pitfall before the feet of any Christian novelist is the temptation to produce propaganda, where the narrative simply serves an end, and both action and characters are selected to make a point. The problem here is that the characters simply become puppets, without a life of their own. I wanted to encourage novelists who can tell a rattling good tale, a story which makes their readers aware of what is true and false, noble and mean; which fosters compassion for the creatures of the world, including its human creatures; which opens hearts and minds to new possibilities, and the hidden potency of the One who knows and names all.

My heroes in this enterprise were, and remain, the obvious culprits: C.S. Lewis and J.R.R. Tolkien and Dorothy L. Sayers; and fellow travellers who do not profess any faith, to my knowledge, but who stand on truth and acutely observe the human condition: writers such as Ursula LeGuin, Jim Butcher, Robertson Davies, Julian May, and Patrick O'Brian.

Fiction publishing, however, requires a *huge* investment of time, from author and publisher alike.

To write a good work of nonfiction needs patience, a keen mind, a knowledge of your subject, a facility with words, an engaging personality, and a grasp of what will keep a reader's attention.

To write a good work of fiction you should add to the mix: an intuitive perception of what makes people tick; an understanding of the evolution of character; a sure grip on nuance and subtlety; an ear for dialogue; a poet's grasp of metaphor; and the capacity to weave a good tale.

To edit any book requires an empathy for the author, an ear for the cadence of language, painstaking attention to detail, a logical mind, and an ability to see the big picture.

Fiction requires all this, and more. Imagine conducting an orchestra, where the woodwinds may at any moment start playing in a minor key, the first violin has omitted to tune her instrument, and the percussion section has a mind all its own. To edit a novel you have to savour each snatch of dialogue, probe every interaction. Would she have said that? Why did he react that way? The editor requires both confidence and humility, because you are working with another's child, in a way that is more intimate and personal than is usually the case with nonfiction.

It is also far harder to assess for publication an unsolicited novel than an unsolicited work of nonfiction. With theology or popular spirituality, for instance, it is usually fairly clear, and fairly quickly, whether or not the author knows their field, whether they can write, and whether anyone is likely to be interested in what they have to say. As Edward England advised me early on, you start by sniffing.

With novels, too, if you are simply glancing at a submission with the expectation of turning it down, that's relatively easy. The brutal truth is that if the first two pages do not hold you, the next three hundred are not likely to correct the first impression.

The problem comes when the first two pages *do* capture your attention.

With fiction, it is far harder to discern the scent of success. You cannot reliably skim a novel in which you are planning to invest. If you do, not only are you likely to overlook the point at which someone starts to act out of character, you may also miss the fateful lines of dialogue in which the narrative demands something fruitier than 'bother', or the page where the relationship between the hero and heroine progresses further than a chaste kiss. As a publisher, you really do have to know your customers, and two of the biggest no-nos in the Christian sector are sex and bad language. It's not just Christians who are sensitive to such matters, of course, and the BBC regularly fields complaints about swearing. But publishing is about trust, and once your books start to be regarded with suspicion by your marketplace, you are sunk.

Apart from spotting the dodgy bits, you are also looking for the good stuff, the riveting plots, the character evolution, the wit, the depth of insight, the exuberance of living, the capacity to convey their fear as the children realise no help will come. There are questions of pace: does the novel sag in the middle, like a badly made cake? Is the ending a triumphant denouement, or an incoherent whimper? None of this can be assessed swiftly.

You are also hoping to discover a confident, modulated authorial voice, but that develops over time. Few first novels are as polished as their author's third. But someone has to give first novels a chance.

The dollar signs start to tick over when you suspect that there might be something with a pulse before you. At that point you start investing emotionally and intellectually in the book.

Jane and I had been introduced, through an American friend, to the novelist Davis Bunn and his wife Isabella.

Davis and Isabella define American glamour – tall, lean, beautiful, amazingly accomplished, and astonishingly good company. Davis had turned away from a glittering business career to write full time. Isabella is an eminent lawyer. They divide their time between the US and UK. With no family of their own, they delighted in spoiling our two young daughters.

In the spring of 1992, soon after we had purchased Monarch, Davis and Isabella invited Jane and me to spend the night with them at their house in Oxfordshire. More accurately, at their house, on an island, in the middle of the Thames. Davis gave us instructions about which wharf to find, and rowed us across to the jetty next to their home.

Isabella is a fine cook. We were thoroughly pampered.

Davis, who was not in the best health, needed to retire early. Explaining his reasons – he had contracted an infection during a trip to Eastern Europe – he proffered a thin sheet of papers. 'This is a bit different from my usual stuff,' he told us. 'Could you tell me what you think?'

After he and Isabella had retired for the night, Jane and I sat on the couch and started to read, passing pages from one to the other.

The Quilt tells the story of Mary, an elderly grandmother, who is convinced God has one last task for her before he calls her home. Over the course of her life she has made many quilts. Now, she believes, she must make one more, by convening a quilting bee.

A quilting bee is a cheerful, gregarious affair, bringing together a group of quilters to laugh and gossip as they work.

Mary wanted something different. She put out the call for her family and friends to come and help her: she would provide the house and the fabric, but others must sew, as her eyes had grown weak. There was a condition, however. There was to be no conversation. Instead, as the ladies of the gathering created the quilt, every stitch was to be a prayer of thanksgiving.

By midnight Jane and I had finished reading, and looked at each other. We knew we had encountered something holy. Davis was by this point an established writer, versed in plot and intrigue, well known for his pacy, engaging stories. But this was different: a quiet, understated, tightly focused little gem.

Over breakfast the following morning we congratulated him, asking how he had come to write the book. He grinned. What follows is his own account:

Six months before Isabella and I married, my mother's mother started work on a quilt for us as a wedding present. But then she had her stroke, and sewing became impossible. Someone from her home town of Smithfield heard about this, and volunteered to help. Over the next several months my grandmother's last work was passed from one quilting group to another, until it was finished and sent to us three weeks after our wedding.

When the gift arrived in Germany and Isabella started to open the box, I experienced an incredibly intense sensation that my grandmother was there in the room with us. I immediately asked Isabella to stop what she was doing, as I wanted to capture this sensation on the page. I took the unopened box into my study, and spent the next six weeks writing the story. Only when my novella was finished did I let Isabella see our wedding gift.

We had to postpone our honeymoon because we were both working on very tight schedules. Three months later, we flew first to Minneapolis and met with the publishers of my first book. Then we flew to Hawaii.

On the flight from Europe, I gave Isabella the text of *The Quilt*.

Isabella just bawled.

The stewardesses knew we were going on our honeymoon, and assumed I had done something awful to upset my new bride. They gave Isabella several bottles of champagne and refused to speak to me for the rest of the transatlantic flight.[55]

When we landed in Minneapolis, Isabella insisted that I send my grandmother the story. She refused to wait until we arrived in North Carolina, the last stop on our journey, and allow me to hand-deliver it. She was absolutely certain that my grandmother needed to see this now.

Then on our return from Hawaii, at a stopover in Saint Louis, I phoned my sister to say that our flight had been delayed. She told me that my grandmother had passed on, and the funeral was that very day.

We went straight from Raleigh airport to the church.

---

55. 'It was a long time to go without food and water,' observed Davis.

After the service, people started coming up to us, embracing us both, and telling us how *The Quilt* had become the last thing my grandmother read before she passed on. In her final days speech became quite difficult. So when friends and family came to visit, she asked them to read to her from the manuscript.

The story might well have ended here. And it did, for five long years.

The Quilt was too short to be published as a novel, and too long to sell as a short story. It occupied a nebulous world of strong emotions and sentimentality, and I was developing a reputation as a writer of mysteries and contemporary drama.

Five years.

Soon after the Iron Curtain came crashing down, my wife and I travelled to Eastern Europe so that I might research the second of a trilogy based in Poland, the former East Germany, and the Ukraine. I came down with an amoebic infection of my liver and gall bladder that rendered me exhausted for almost three months. During that time, my new British publisher came for the weekend, and since I was going to bed around five in the afternoon, I gave them this manuscript to read. Why exactly I chose this story, I have no idea.

Two days later, they called and offered me a contract.

Davis generously gave us British rights, and *The Quilt* was released a few months later.

Isabella, who doubled as her husband's literary agent, sold American rights to Bethany House Publishers.

To our distress and embarrassment, the Monarch edition didn't make the impact we had hoped. 'Christian fiction' had not really made the giant step across the Atlantic, and we lacked the resources to overcome customers' indifference.

The Bethany edition succeeded, brilliantly. Released as a pleasing small hardback, it was taken up by Hallmark (publishers of the famous cards) and sold hundreds of thousands. A couple of decades later it was reissued as a coffee-table gift book. It remains one of Davis's most popular novels.

There is a genre of North American fiction called 'prairie romances': tales of the heart, set in the Western states. One of the first, and greatest, exponents is a lovely lady called Janette Oke. A Canadian author of inspirational fiction, she writes emotionally involving stories about frontier life.

Carol Johnson, editorial director of Bethany House, who had suggested that Davis Bunn and I might find common ground, proposed I should take a look at *Love Comes Softly*, Janette's first novel.

Frontier romances are scarcely my standard reading, but I was utterly charmed by the story of the marriage of stark convenience undertaken on the prairies in the mid-1800s by Marty and Clark Davis.

It's probably unwise to sign contracts when you don't know what you are doing. The book itself was gold dust – the American edition has sold over a million copies, spawned seven sequels, and was made into a film – but I had no inkling how to sell romantic novels; the cultural assumptions were a world removed not only from my own, but from most British readers; the book was unashamedly sentimental, and contained not a trace of the scepticism so characteristic of British taste; the author was unknown to British audiences. I tried in vain to persuade bookshop managers and editors of magazines that *Love Comes Softly* was worth reading and supporting. A chimpanzee would have had better luck explaining the finer points of Mozart. Friends looked upon me with pity, and crossed the street when they saw me coming.[56]

Entirely predictably, the Monarch edition of this excellent novel also failed.

Two such disappointments in quick succession left me with the false impression that there was not a sufficient market in the UK for Christian novels. The Peretti novels had been a blip, I concluded, read for their spiritual content rather than as good stories. Then there was the business aspect. I could sell three times as many copies of a book on church planting as any of these novels.[57]

Gloomily I abandoned thoughts of a fiction programme for the next decade.

I didn't come back to fiction until the early 2000s, when a chance conversation at an American book fair drew my attention to *Redeeming Love* by Francine Rivers.

Francine Rivers is a master storyteller, who had enjoyed ten years of success as a writer of historical romances before she became a Christian. Wanting to turn her craft

---

56. Ok, not really. But their eyes did glaze over.
57. Quite literally. *Planting Tomorrow's Churches Today* by Martin Robinson and Stuart Christine did particularly well.

to the service of her new-found faith, she spent years studying the Bible before deciding to focus on the Old Testament book of Hosea, which recounts how God told the prophet Hosea to marry a prostitute, Gomer. Her first novel after her conversion was *Redeeming Love*. Set during the Californian Gold Rush, the book tells how Angel, a cynical hooker, eventually finds faith and hope through the patience and love of a frontier farmer, Michael Hosea. In Francine Rivers' capable hands, the sacrificial love story rings true.

Redeeming Love was released in 1991. The American company Tyndale, which would become her primary publisher, rejected *Redeeming Love* because it was a little too bold for their readership. The book was published instead by Multnomah, who found a winner on their hands.

Twelve years later I was chatting to the senior editor at Multnomah during the International Christian Retail Show, held each year in the States. 'You do realise,' he commented as we finished our conversation, 'that *Redeeming Love* has never been published in Britain?'

At my raised eyebrow he dragged me over to his booth, and pressed a reading copy into my hands. On the plane home I fished it out of my bag, and was transfixed.

Francine Rivers has written a number of subsequent novels, which have done well and won many awards. *Redeeming Love* remains her masterpiece. She used her capacity to create character and spin a good yarn to excellent effect, and the arresting Old Testament narrative of redemption which lies behind her book provides hope and inspiration. Many works of Christian fiction really appeal mainly to the tastes of the saved. *Redeeming Love* achieves the goal so frequently missed: that of telling a grand story in a way that a reader without an iota of faith or a smidgeon of biblical knowledge, would find compelling. 'The most powerful work of fiction you will ever read,' said Liz Curtis Higgs, herself a million-selling novelist.

Nick Jones was worried. Aware of the reputation Rivers enjoyed, he quizzed me about the advance I had in mind. I had my own past bruises from American fiction. 'We'll offer £1,000,' I told him. 'If we can't afford what they ask we'll just walk away.'

Rather to our surprise, Multnomah accepted our bid, only stipulating that the contract should be renegotiated every five years.

We didn't greatly admire the American cover, and Roger Chouler came up with a far more arresting alternative (which Multnomah subsequently emulated).

So, years after its American publication, *Redeeming Love* was presented to British readers. We didn't want to commit major resources to its release, but we did what we could. We were caught up at that point in negotiations with Lion.

To say the British edition was happily received is laughably inadequate. It fared so well that, a decade later, it became the foundation stone of a new imprint, Lion Fiction. Jaw-dropping royalty cheques started flowing from England to America. When the second contractual renewal came around, Multnomah informed us that, if we wished to retain rights for the next five years, the price would be £20,000. We paid without hesitation.

The book is now a major film.

Lots of publishers had missed it. If it had not been for a casual remark, I would have missed it too.

Why, though, did *Redeeming Love* succeed so spectacularly, when a decade earlier *Loves Comes Softly* had failed? Both are American historical romances, both cast in an authentic and well-evoked context, both set in periods celebrated in song and story. Both are fine books.

At least part of the answer lies in the influence of the publisher. Monarch, under Angus Hudson, and even more so under Lion Hudson, was a more considerable force than its earlier self. But the history of publishing is littered with examples of books from small houses hitting the headlines.

Perhaps, a decade on, the Christian market had a greater appetite for fiction?

I think the answer may lie in a difference of mindset. As discussed earlier, American Christians, especially in the conservative heartlands, are more steeped in a cultural worldview where faith is the foundation. British Christians – and Christians in many other parts of the world – rub shoulders daily with a secular majority who regard their beliefs as an oddity, and the perspective is catching. *Redeeming Love* is particularly accessible to those without faith.

In the summer of 2006, through a mutual friend, I received a note from an unknown writer in the States. With it came a first draft of a first novel, a medieval whodunit, *The Unquiet Bones*.

Mel Starr, a retired history teacher from Michigan, had gone through a long apprenticeship, attending writing classes and knocking on the doors of publishers and agents right across America. Rejection followed rejection.

The character he had created – prompted by an overnight stay in an Oxfordshire village – was Hugh de Singleton, Surgeon. Here is the introduction from Mel's website:

Hugh of Singleton, fourth son of a minor knight in Wyclif's England, has been educated as a clerk, usually a prelude to taking holy orders. However, feeling no certain calling despite a lively faith, he turns to the profession of surgeon, training in Paris and then hanging out his sign in Oxford. He was staring from his Oxford window, hoping for clients, when Lord Gilbert was kicked by his groom's horse. Hugh's successful treatment of the suffering lord led to an invitation to set up his practice in the village of Bampton – and, before long, the request to track the killer of a young woman whose bones have been found in the castle cesspit. She is identified as the impetuous missing daughter of a local blacksmith, and her young man, whom she had provoked very publicly, is in due course arrested and sentenced at the Oxford assizes. From there the tale unfolds, with graphic medical procedures, droll medieval wit, misdirection, ambition, romantic distractions and a consistent underlying Christian compassion.[58]

One of the first questions an editor must ask of an author is: do they know their stuff? It was evident from the first

---

58. www.melstarr.net

page that Mel had convincingly caught and rendered into prose what sounded like authentic medieval cadences. This isn't easy to do, and historical novels have to offer a sense of entering into an unfamiliar world without sacrificing common ground between reader and subject. For Mel, who had taught high school students for decades, the exercise of translation – of standing between present and past – was meat and drink.

He also wanted to bring into play characters for whom faith is part of the fabric of their lives. At that point in English history the spiritual realm infused the imagination of the culture, creating motivation and a frame of reference. Hugh de Singleton might reasonably mutter a prayer without inducing a sense of unreality in the reader.

The book appealed, but I wasn't sure, so gave it to Pen to read. Pen is not given to easy praise, but she really liked it. Encouraged, I began the long process of building a presentation to my colleagues – summary, potential readership, author profile, accurate and credible comparisons with other books, marketing ideas, schedule, format and price, costs, projected income. I had a team to persuade, and first novels by retired American teachers are not at the head of the queue when it comes to the investment of scarce resources. It is also unrealistic to expect your preoccupied co-workers to read every proposal themselves: editors are expected to undertake the donkeywork and present a viable business case.

It took months of discussion, persuasion, and casual mentions over lunch. In the world of editorial judgement, sustained enthusiasm counts for something, but if you back too many wild horses your credibility quickly sinks.

Yet I had thoroughly enjoyed the book, and gradually I won my colleagues round. Nick Jones in particular was hard to please: 'I don't like the title,' he muttered, as he saw grudging assent starting to build.

Through all this, I had an anxious Mel Starr emailing me regularly for updates. On the day I told him the good news I could sense his grin across the ether. 'If this works,' he told me, 'I'm going to buy myself a Corvette Stingray.' The elegant, dramatically styled sports car is the stuff of many a driver's dreams.

The plot was intriguing, the characters engaging, the period detail beguiling. But it was still a first novel, and rough around the edges. I asked Jan Greenough, who had done such a fine job with Angus Buchan (and who boasted an MA in English literature) to scrutinise the text at close quarters, deal with some lacunae, and polish the whole.

We published *The Unquiet Bones* in 2008. The first Chronicle of Hugh de Singleton, Surgeon, has been followed by many more. Mel is disciplined and industrious, draws upon decades of study, and knows what makes a good yarn.

A few years later he sent me a photo of himself, driving through the main street of his town in Michigan, at the wheel of his bright red Corvette Stingray.

Over the next few years we published a steady trickle of novels under the Monarch label. Some did well. But it became clear that you could not dabble in this field: you had to commit. In 2013, the company launched a new imprint, Lion Fiction.

Our objective was not to emulate our publishing cousins across the Atlantic, from whom a steady stream of inspirational fiction flows for Christian consumption. We wanted to do something different, to publish novels with an underlying Christian worldview but without a Christian agenda, for consumption by a wider reading public. In trying to set out our stall I often fell back on a metaphor: we wanted to till the ground so that the seed might be sown. But this was not the clear endorsement of faith that some sought, and we were aware we were moving beyond the comfort zone of many Christian bookshops, and indeed of many Christians.

All publishing is an act of faith.

Shortly after the new imprint was announced, the distinguished agent Pieter Kwant (who had placed with us *The Heavenly Man*), sent me the first draft of *The Heretic* by Henry Vyner-Brooks. Vyner-Brooks was a novelist, landscape architect, filmmaker, property developer, and more. Acutely intelligent, he was also profoundly dyslexic – but boy, could he tell a story.

His novel was set in 1536: a year when strange ideas intrude, strange lands are discovered, and the king's dissolution of the monasteries is overturning the customs and authorities of centuries. In the new world order, spies abound, and no one can be trusted. For Brother Pacificus of the Abbey of St Benet's in Norfolk, it seems as if his abbey alone will be spared. But this last Benedictine house is mired in murder and intrigue, some of it linked to Brother Pacificus's own warlike past.

Based on historical events, this post-medieval mystery is laced with romance, fuelled by greed, and offers a tale of redemption for some. It's a grand, complex, satisfying read, and a long one (the paperback runs to over six hundred pages).

I could see why Pieter was keen, but would the game be worth the candle? Confidence buoyed by the zest of the new imprint, I persuaded my colleagues that this was a book to be placed alongside the Thomas Cromwell novels of Hilary Mantel and the historical fiction of C.J. Sansom – both riding very high at that point.

It required a monumental amount of editing, a task I entrusted to Pen: the task took months, and required the careful correction of historical errors. She did a fine job, and the completed novel is compelling reading.

Our design team created an outstanding cover.

To my chagrin, and the dismay of both author and colleagues, *The Heretic* made no impact at all. It garnered some excellent reviews, but the blunt fact is that launching a new novelist, even one as charismatic and engaging as Henry, requires major investment and exceptionally adroit marketing. Publishing can be frustrating, and heart-breaking, and expensive.

It remains a fine book.

Earlier I mentioned Pen's Hawk and Dove trilogy. This had stuttered to a stop in the UK, but was enjoying a decades-long shelf life with Crossway in the States, who had bought world rights and combined the first three volumes into one substantial tome.

Set in fourteenth century North Yorkshire, the novels introduce us to the monks of St Alcuin's Abbey, and Abbot Peregrine – an impatient, arrogant, decisive man who, over the course of the first three novels, learns compassion and gains the grace to accept affection.

Pen stopped the series in 1991, after this trilogy. Then, with the twentieth anniversary of the first book approaching, she asked Crossway if they'd like to celebrate that with a subsequent volume, after which the tale grew in the telling. Pen returned to her monks and wrote volumes four to six, which Crossway also released, in editions aimed at the American market. There's a writing gap of nearly two decades between *The Hawk and the Dove* and the fourth volume, *The Hardest Thing to Do*, which picks up the story of St Alcuin's a year later when an old enemy of Peregrine's resurfaces – Prior William de Bulmer, the arch-schemer with scary eyes.

When Crossway finally decided to pack in their fiction programme, Pen self-published the seventh in the series, *The Breath of Peace*. Then Lion Fiction came on the scene, picking up volume seven and the others she wanted to write. Crossway, in an act of true generosity, relinquished all rights, and we set to work to create a series 'look', to reissue the first six, and to bring out the last three titles.

A medieval monastery is in some respects quite basic. The food is bread and beans, travel is on foot or by ox cart, monks sit by the fire and chat when the day's work is ended. The pattern of worship sets the rhythm of the day. They sleep in stone cells. This is an accessible compass, where simplicity gives rise to nuance. Mostly set within a single monastery, the novels concern a handful of characters. The plots are straightforward, but the themes are universal.

Readers from around the world still write telling her of faith deepened, hope regained. 'I think the series achieved what I set out to do,' she observes. 'It enables people to grasp imaginatively how life might be if we lived as Christians. I wrote to make goodness attractive. These are stories about people doing their best.'

The ninth and last volume, *A Day and a Life*, appeared in 2016.

14

After

I stepped back from running Monarch and Lion Fiction in 2015, having finally achieved my bus pass. Pleased to be free of the weekly slog between Hastings and Oxford, I continued working part-time.

The last few years at the company had been turbulent. Nick Jones had taken on the position of MD after Paul Clifford retired in 2012, but Nick's own health was fragile (an absurd word to use of such a force of nature) and he spent more and more time working from home as the headaches worsened. In the summer of 2016 he decided to retire. Carol, who for many years had been at the helm of the Candle imprint, elected to do likewise: the company could ill afford to lose such able players.

Suzanne Wilson-Higgins, the sales director, stepped into Nick's shoes as MD.

Paul Clifford's place as editorial director (he had worn both hats) had been taken by Andrew Hodder-Williams, a scion of the Hodder family. A successful publishing consultant, Andrew set to with a will, but he arrived at a tricky time.

The company was stuttering. The co-edition aspect, on which its prosperity had been built, was no longer such a cash cow, as new technology freed our overseas publishing partners to devise their own material. Children's books often need expensive artwork, which requires high print runs to achieve a sensible unit cost. Margins were thinning, stocks were mounting.

Concurrently a new computer system – that traditional slayer of businesses – was costing hundreds of thousands of pounds as the software developers struggled to replicate Lion Hudson's complex operating model.

Cash was tight, and grew tighter.

In August 2016 Peter Martin rang. Peter was chief executive of Spring Harvest, a shrewd, incisive and hard-working leader, and a man of prayer. I had looked after the Spring Harvest account for some years, and he and I had become friends.

Peter and Nick had been close – almost brothers – for decades, sharing advice, woes, jokes, and not infrequently a round of golf.

Now Peter's cheery voice was choked. 'Nick's gone,' he blurted.

Nick had stayed indoors one morning at their home near Bath while Carol worked in the garden. She returned to the house to find him lying dead on the sofa. The cause of death was unclear. That great frame, that acute intelligence, that abundant and generous spirit: all vanished. He died just a month after he had retired.

Messages of regret poured in, reflecting the shock of the Christian publishing community. He had been so widely loved. I edited the many condolences into a book, which was handed out at the service at St Aldates Oxford celebrating his life. George Verwer, who had played such a part in Nick's path to faith, led the tributes.

On 30 January 2017, I lifted the phone to hear an unfamiliar voice informing me that Lion Hudson plc had gone into administration. I, and more than thirty others, were being made redundant. Suzanne and a small team would stay on to salvage what they could, and ultimately to rebuild.

In any company collapse the primary cost is human.

The team at Lion Hudson was remarkably capable: a select band of designers, sales people, production managers, administrators, editors. Many were young, with weighty mortgages and dependent families. The corporate culture was one of mutual support, of creativity and engagement, of joint effort in the service of a shared dream. Now that concentrated talent drained away.

Lion Hudson owed significant sums to printers, mainly in the Far East. They were some of the primary creditors, but there were lots of small traders and freelancers who had stuck with Lion Hudson as payment days came, and went. Many lost out.

Shops which had relied on Lion Hudson's output, particularly their children's books, were left wondering what would happen.

Authors who had hoped to see their titles launched with verve and panache found phone calls were not returned.

The administrators sought a purchaser, but the debts were formidable.

Ultimately David Dorricott stepped in. David – a software billionaire and philanthropist – had already supported Lion Hudson generously, and now he purchased the whole, transferring it to limited company status, ensuring authors were paid their royalties, and supporting Suzanne and her little team as they tried to rebuild the publishing programme.

The remainder of the staff had no option but to dust off their CVs and start applying for jobs. It is a measure of their ability that most found positions in weeks. A few elected to retire: some used their redundancy payment to set themselves up as freelancers.

Lion Hudson pulled through, with David's stalwart support, and began to rebuild their publishing programme.

To my surprise and pleasure, Sam Richardson, the chief executive of SPCK, invited me for an interview and offered a part-time role as editor at large, a title I had had latterly at Lion Hudson.

SPCK is one of the world's oldest publishers, founded in 1698 – nearly a hundred years before the French Revolution, to give it some context. Its long and complex history is inseparable from British culture. Throughout the eighteenth century, SPCK was by far the largest producer of Christian literature in Britain. It is the oldest Anglican mission organisation in the world, with a long history of training and resourcing clergy worldwide. Despite its venerable roots, SPCK today is a dynamic operation, with a startlingly eclectic list of authors ranging from the liberal and Catholic to the conservative and evangelical.

To play a role at SPCK was a privilege, and a most congenial way to round off a publishing career. I finally stepped down at Christmas 2019.

A few conclusions.

A book is a private engagement between two people. If your habit of speech is locked in broadcast mode, don't be surprised if your reader walks away. A book is a relationship. You write for one person at a time.

The author is a guest at their reader's table. A book is rarely consumed at a single sitting, so your first task as an author is to ensure you are sufficiently congenial company to be invited back.

Write so compellingly your reader misses their train.

Surprise your reader.

Part of your role is to entertain.

Most books are sold by word of mouth, and few will recommend a book unless they have finished it. Sustain the energy. Ensure your reader wants to drain the last drop. A friend in the Association of Christian Writers drew my attention to an essay by William Golding, called 'Rough Magic', in which Golding observes, 'Have one hand on your pen and the other firmly on the nape of the reader's neck. That is rule one, to which everything else must be sacrificed. Once you have got him, never let him go.'[59]

If you are a publisher, or an editor, remember that to be an author is a lonely calling. Even the simplest book will be the outcome of tens of solitary hours at the keyboard.

---

59. The essay is part of a collection called *A Moving Target*, published by Faber and Faber.

Authors appreciate contact with their publisher. Books are not products: they are written in blood and silence. So don't forget to reply to emails, or to return phone calls. Don't keep authors waiting.

If you are an author, bear in mind that no matter how genial or smooth an editor may be, they have to hit financial targets. You need them to hit those targets, or poof, no more publisher. The urgency of your conviction won't translate to their bottom line. The quality of your book may.

A lot of publishing is about timing, and anticipation. The ancient Greeks had two words for time: *chronos*, time passing, traditionally depicted as an old man with lantern and scythe, a figure of death; and *kairos*, time as opportunity, depicted as a lithe winged youth. Kairos has a full head of hair to the crown, but behind the ears he is bald: you may seize him as he dashes towards you, but once he is past you will grasp at him uselessly. The moment is gone.

Every book is a risk. It is a risk to write it, because you don't know whether anyone will care enough to open the cover. It is an expensive risk to read it, because you open the blinds of your mind not knowing what may creep in. It is a critically expensive risk to publish it, because it may make you rich, or bankrupt you. Any book teeters on the edge of failure. Which is why publishing is so much fun.

If you put your head above the spiritual parapet, as I have observed, you are likely to attract hostile fire. This is acutely true if you are also in a position of leadership. Do you have those around you who will pray for you, laugh with you, speak truth to you, and boost your spirits when the clouds gather?

Publishers and editors are not exempt.

If you are a publisher, pray for your authors. If you are an author, pray for your readers. If you are a reader, thank the Almighty for both.

You cannot control how people will respond. They may pass by with indifference, they may be incensed, they may steal your ideas, they may mock, or kneel and pray.

It is the nature of publishing that you learn on the job. There are constants, of course, but like many of the creative industries, every day is new. Each book is different, as is each author, and it is foolish to think you have mastered the art. You do, genuinely, have to start by listening. Unless you pay proper attention, you will miss the unique quality – the flavour – which makes a book special.

If, having paid attention, you still find a book disappointingly bland, then you are not the right publisher. It's possible, of course, that there isn't one.

Was it all worthwhile?

Oh yes.

As an editor, as a publisher, you get to rub shoulders with the best and worst. I have met people for whom the publisher was little more than a vanity mirror, expected to smooth into place the stray hairs on their ego. Christian ministry does attract its share of narcissists, whose delight is to watch themselves being humble.

But I have also met people who forgave the most egregious transgressions, of which some have been mine. I have met women and men of profound faith, and generous spirit, and dogged endurance; scholars of shining intellect; those whom the Spirit filled; whose capacity for taking risks permitted the creation of an enduring vision; whose joy set alight the hearts of those around them; ordinary human beings lifted above the ordinary by their capacity for caring when others would have quit. It has been my privilege to help them write their books, and to publish them.

As a publisher you can never really know whether your work will prove to be of gold, or of straw. Under the Mercy – and it is a mercy – you cannot be sure whether this book or that will speak enduring truth; whether this author or another is someone into whose work you should pour your time and love. All you can ever do, at the start of another business day, is to try and reorient yourself True North, to ensure your armour of light fits snugly around your shoulders, and then to sally forth, one hand on your sword and the other on your calculator.

As I was drafting the final chapters of this book, news came through that planning permission had been granted for construction of the Eternal Wall of Answered Prayer, near Birmingham. It is the brainchild of Richard Gamble.

Richard is an entrepreneur, with a successful career in business and the charity sector. He is also a former chaplain of Leicester City Football Club.

In 2004 he was seized with the vision to create a monument honouring the responses of God to his people: specifically, to celebrate answered prayer. As Richard puts it, he wanted 'to make hope visible'; to provoke a national conversation about prayer.

Many would agree, nod sagely, and move on to the next headline.

Richard, however, is a man of passion and drive. He created a team to build the Eternal Wall of Answered Prayer from across the UK, consisting of architects, civil engineers, planning consultants, web developers, social media experts and marketeers. A prominent site outside Birmingham, visible from the M6 and M42 motorways, and close to Birmingham airport and the route of HS2, was donated by Lord Edmiston, a motor trade billionaire and Conservative Party donor. With funding from Kickstarter, Richard commissioned the Royal Institute of British Architects to run a competition for a suitable design. Five were shortlisted, and revealed at an exhibition at the House of Lords.

Richard threw the choice open to the public. The final selection – a swooping, breath-taking infinity loop, a Möbius strip – comprises a million bricks. A striking feature of this huge piece of public art is that tens of thousands of special bricks will each tell a story. By focusing your phone on an individual brick, a specific narrative of answered prayer will appear on your screen. Stories, submitted by the public, are carefully vetted, and drawn from both historical and contemporary accounts.

Plans include an educational exhibition on prayer; interactive touch screens to access answered prayers; a 24/7 prayer room; a café and Christian bookstore; and a park area for prayer and reflection. Trained chaplains will provide support. The project will be built with funding from public donations. Entry for the many expected visitors will be free, but the café, bookshop, and other resources will generate revenue: all profits from its ongoing operation will go to support social housing and other charitable initiatives.

As the plans were announced opposition started to mount – not least from some within the Christian community – and the monument will certainly attract ongoing controversy.

I first heard of the project at Spring Harvest, when Peter Martin introduced me to Mr Gamble. In a café at Butlins I listened with mounting astonishment as Richard, a bearded, positive individual, laid out what seemed at first like a fantasy. By that point he had some serious backers, and my brain started to fizz as the dimensions of the endeavour became clear.

At length Richard sat back. 'It's a big story,' he observed. 'I've already written part of one book. I can think of at least two more.'

I nodded. My mind raced ahead. Apart from the story of the Wall, there would be books collecting together narratives of answered prayer; works of popular theology; a volume of pictures celebrating the construction.

'I've been talking to publishers,' he said bluntly. 'I know it's a risk, and so do they. Everyone is hedging and hesitating. We haven't got planning permission yet. Once we get it' ('*If* you get it,' I amended silently), 'lots of publishers will want to leap on board.' He stared at me. 'I'm looking for a publishing partner who will stand with me now.'

With a private moment of intense intercession, I started asking questions. Who was supporting him, financially and ecclesiastically? Who was providing theological advice? This could be a ready-made opportunity for every crazy-eyed enthusiast: who would collect the stories, and how would they be selected and checked? Would he include stories from non-Christian sources? We were meeting at an evangelical event: would there be stories from all Christian traditions, including the Catholics and Orthodox? What about stories of *un*answered prayer?

It was quickly evident Richard had done his thinking, and was candid in his responses. As we talked, I decided this was one proposal I should definitely take to SPCK.

My colleagues, experienced editors and marketeers and sales folk, quickly grasped the scale of the opportunity – and the degree of risk. The debate swung back and forth, at meeting after meeting. Other major publishers had turned the book down. SPCK have a deserved reputation as a safe pair of hands. They are good at what they do. They publish for bishops and archbishops. They think things through. You don't survive for over three hundred years by taking foolish risks. SPCK's participation would add plausibility: such support cannot be offered lightly.

Equally importantly, how could you write any kind of budget for such a book? Any sales projection would be a work of fiction. If the project went ahead, any book associated with it might be wildly popular. If planning permission was refused, the book would still be under contract, an embarrassing and costly turkey.

Yet this was not the whole picture. SPCK takes its role as a publisher of faith entirely seriously. One of its most commendable policies, initiated by Sam Richardson, the chief executive, and Philip Law, the publishing director, is that it allows each editor one 'wild card' each year: a book which doesn't meet the standard parameters, but which the company will get behind nevertheless. The policy – similar to the climate of innovation at Apple – allows staff to have ideas, and to fail, without recrimination. It also allows an important space for new authors.

In any creative industry you have to be allowed to make mistakes. Not all ideas pan out. You never have enough data. You make decisions based on shifting imponderables. Enthusiasm is often costly, but without it you follow the well-trodden path to mediocrity.

'You haven't yet used your wild card this year,' commented Philip. 'Do you want to play it?'

I did.

Tony Collins tried retiring, but it didn't stick.
He is now a literary agent.

Postscript

In 2021 Lion Hudson was acquired by SPCK, which had also acquired IVP UK a few years before. The combined business holds considerable potential, with a substantial and valuable backlist and a spectrum of publishing imprints. The acquisition marks an important milestone in the evolution of Christian publishing in the UK.

Acknowledgments

This stumbling account omits many friends, and many authors (the two often overlap, to my delight).

Let me briefly pay tribute here to just a few.

Catherine Campbell, former nurse, now a hugely popular author, approached me after a meeting of the Association of Christian Writers. Catherine has a particular gift for bringing the wisdom of the Bible to bear on daily life. Catherine and her pastor husband are no strangers to tragedy, but Catherine has transmuted her grief into compassion. One of her titles has won Christian Book of the Year. She is also a smashing speaker.

Canon Andrew White (formerly known as 'the Vicar of Baghdad') was first introduced to me by a friend, Chris Mungeam. For decades Andrew has played a valuable role in the ministry of reconciliation in the Middle East. Trusted by men who trust very few, he has an unusual gift for friendship. Largely confined to a wheelchair by advancing MS, he continues to exercise an international ministry.

Dr Andy Bannister, his wife Astrid, Pen, and I shared a house group for years. Andy has a doctorate in Islamic studies, but his first calling is as an evangelist. Swift of mind, subversively witty, and author of several acclaimed books, he has a spectacular following on Twitter, and adores daft footnotes.

Paul Hattaway and I have spoken, but never met. Author of *The Heavenly Man*, he once sent me a photo of himself – taken with a standard lens from a mile or more away across a mountainside. Paul, an authority on Chinese life and culture, makes regular visits to China to connect with believers, and for reasons of discretion makes no public appearances. A careful but prolific writer, he is currently engaged on a multi-volume history of the modern Chinese Church.

The Revd Dr Mark Stibbe combines a fine mind with a whimsical sense of humour, and is the author of many excellent books. He and the evangelist J.John collaborated on a series of what were ostensibly preaching resources, but were in truth engaging collections of quips and good stories. The first, *A Box of Delights*, included a variant on the Lord's Prayer which provoked a complaint from the Prayer Book Society – which led in turn to a gratifying half-page feature in the *Sunday Telegraph*. Mark is now a professional writer and trainer of writers.

Over the years I have worked with many valuable colleagues and friends, too many to list, but let me give a particular shout out to some who have been my closest collaborators in the exhilarating world of books: Geoff Booker; Paul Bootes; Becki Bradshaw; Peter Brierley; Roger and Christine Chouler; Paul Clifford; Simon Cox; Jess Gladwell; Steve Goss; Jan Greenough; Wendy Grisham; Richard Herkes; Bettina Heynes; Dave Hill; Dennis Hillman; Ali Hull; Carol Jones; Philip Law; Chip MacGregor; Peter Martin; Richard Martin; Jenny Muscat; Jane Pendarves; Sam Richardson; Jonathan Roberts; Rod Shepherd; Eleanor

Trotter; Tony Wales; Rob Wendover; Andrew Wormleighton. I have learned so much from you all.

A particular doff of the cap to Ali Hull, who copy-edited this book shrewdly and rigorously; to Louise Stenhouse, who gave the text a final polish, and saved me from an especially stupid error; and to Malcolm Down and Sarah Grace, who took a risk on this book, and handled the publishing process with skill and care.

To John Maust, president of Media Associates International, a special thank you for planting the seed of this book.